At Issue

| Animal Experimentation

Other Books in the At Issue Series:

At Issue

| Animal Experimentation

Susan Hunnicutt, Book Editor

GREENHAVEN PRESS
A part of Gale, Cengage Learning

GALE
CENGAGE Learning·

Detroit • New York • San Francisco • New Haven, Conn • Waterville, Maine • London

Elizabeth Des Chenes, *Director, Publishing Solutions*

For more information, contact:
Greenhaven Press
27500 Drake Rd.
Farmington Hills, MI 48331-3535
Or you can visit our Internet site at gale.cengage.com

For product information and technology assistance, contact us at

Gale Customer Support, 1-800-877-4253
For permission to use material from this text or product, submit all requests online at www.cengage.com/permissions

Further permissions questions can be emailed to permissionrequest@cengage.com

Articles in Greenhaven Press anthologies are often edited for length to meet page requirements. In addition, original titles of these works are changed to clearly present the main thesis and to explicitly indicate the author's opinion. Every effort is made to ensure that Greenhaven Press accurately reflects the original intent of the authors. Every effort has been made to trace the owners of copyrighted material.

Cover image © Images.com/Corbis.

LIBRARY OF CONGRESS CATALOGING-IN-PUBLICATION DATA

Animal experimentation / Susan Hunnicutt, book editor.
    p. cm. -- (At issue)
  Includes bibliographical references and index.
  ISBN 978-0-7377-6143-6 (hardcover) -- ISBN 978-0-7377-6144-3 (pbk.)
  1. Animal experimentation. 2. Animal experimentation--Moral and ethical
aspects. 3. Animal rights. I. Hunnicutt, Susan.
  HV4915.A6363 2013
  179'.4--dc23
                                                              2012048711

Printed in the United States of America
1 2 3 4 5 6 7 17 16 15 14 13

Contents

Introduction

In April 2011, Maria Cantwell, a Democrat from Washington, introduced S. 810, the Great Ape Protection and Cost Savings Act of 2011, in the US Senate. If passed, the bill would prohibit medical researchers in the United States from possessing great apes—chimpanzees, bonobos, gorillas, orangutans, and gibbons—for the purposes of medical research, and it would make it illegal for researchers to conduct invasive research on them. Drug testing, isolation, and social deprivation would be prohibited. The legislation would also outlaw use of federal funds for the care or breeding of great apes in connection with scientific research, and it would protect apes currently in the custody of the federal government by prohibiting transfer of ownership to a private facility engaged in invasive scientific research. The Secretary of Health and Human Services would be required to retire all chimpanzees in the custody of the federal government (in April 2011 there were about five hundred). Finally, the act would create a fund within the Department of the Treasury for the purposes of constructing, maintaining, and operating sanctuary facilities for great apes that would be retired from research.

Few issues are more laden with emotion and controversy than the question of whether apes—and chimpanzees in particular—should continue to be used as subjects in biomedical research. Chimpanzees are the closest living relatives of humans, sharing 96 percent of our DNA, and the chimp genome has become a powerful source of new information about human biology and evolution. This similarity makes chimpanzees exceptionally good models for predicting how humans will respond to new drugs and other treatments. Thomas Rowell, director of New Iberia Research Center, a facility in Louisiana that houses more than seven thousand primates used in medical research, believes that the similarities between chimpanzees and humans make chimpanzees absolutely essential in certain areas of research. He explains in a January 28, 2012, CTV News article, "Some of the products that we work with, for example antibodies, target very specific receptors that are present only on human cells and on chimpanzee cells."

But chimpanzees' similarity to humans is also cited by those who argue that they should be protected. Their highly developed brains, higher level cognitive abilities, and capacity for meaningful social interaction mean that chimpanzees are vulnerable to great suffering when they are confined and subjected to painful and traumatic procedures, as well as when their social relationships are disrupted. A series of case studies of chimpanzees who had been retired from research, published in the *Journal of Trauma and Dissociation* in 2008, found that diagnosis of complex post-traumatic stress disorder (PTSD) in the animals was "consistent with descriptions of trauma-induced symptoms described by the DSM-IV [a publication of the American Psychiatric Association that provides standard criteria for the classification of mental disorders in humans] and human trauma research." In other words, some chimpanzees previously used in biomedical research exhibited symptoms of post-traumatic stress disorder similar to those observed in humans.

Supporters of S. 810 (the legislation proposed by Senator Cantwell) like Michael Markarian, chief operating officer of the Humane Society of the United States, point out that the majority of chimpanzees owned by the federal government and housed in laboratories are not being used in research at all, but instead have been "warehoused," kept in confinement for decades just in case they will be needed in the future. As Markarian noted in an April 13, 2011, Humane Society press release, passing S. 810 "would not only save federal dollars by sending chimpanzees to be cared for in sanctuaries, which are more cost effective than labs, but would also spare these highly intelligent and social creatures from isolation and harm."

As of July 2012, S. 810 had been reported favorably by the Senate Committee on Environment and Public Works, the next step in the process of becoming law. GovTrack.us, an organization that monitors the US legislative process, estimated at that time that the bill had a 28 percent chance of being enacted.

As an alternative to legislation, the National Institutes of Health (NIH) in 2010 ordered a study by the Institute of Medicine (IOM) to determine whether it is scientifically necessary to continue to use chimpanzees for biological or behavioral research. The resulting report noted that while chimpanzees have been valuable in the past, most current use of chimpanzees is not really necessary. However, the report identified several areas where use of the chimpanzees continues to be desirable, including research on monoclonal antibody therapies and comparative genomics. The IOM report also approved of the use of chimpanzees in non-invasive studies looking at social and behavioral factors affecting the development, prevention, and treatment of disease. The committee was divided on the question of whether chimpanzees continue to be needed for studies aimed at developing a vaccine for the hepatitis C virus. It urged the NIH to continue to develop non-chimpanzee models and technologies, but also remained open to the possibility that future research may require the use of chimpanzees.

The IOM recommendations, which were subsequently accepted by the NIH, included three principles for deciding, on a case by case basis, whether to use chimpanzees in future research:

- That the knowledge gained must be necessary to advance the public's health;

- There must be no other research model by which the knowledge could be obtained, and the research cannot be ethically performed on human subjects; and

• The animals used in the proposed research must be maintained either in ethologically appropriate physical and social environments (i.e., as would occur in their natural environment) or in natural habitats.

The IOM has been criticized for its narrow focus on the scientific necessity of using chimpanzees. According to a December 15, 2011, response by the Kennedy Institute of Ethics at Georgetown University, the IOM "never presents a moral justification for conducting research on chimpanzees other than the necessity of their use in order to advance our scientific understanding and to potentially provide benefits to public health. Only human interests play a role in this justification; there is no detailed discussion of the many costs to the chimpanzees as subjects; and, yet, as this IOM Committee correctly notes, the problem of harms to chimpanzees and their moral status is what gave rise to the controversy to which this report is responding."

The question of whether the biomedical research community should continue to employ chimpanzees in its efforts to understand and cure human disease is one of a number of issues emerging from the experimental use of animals. *At Issue: Animal Experimentation* examines several of these issues more closely.

1

Medical Progress Depends on Animal Research

Americans for Medical Progress

Americans for Medical Progress is a nonprofit organization that promotes public understanding of and support for the humane use of animals in medicine.

Animal-based research has led to important advances in the prevention and treatment of many diseases, including cancer, HIV/ AIDS, heart disease, and diabetes. Millions of lives have been saved due to these advances, and further innovations in the coming generations will do even more to improve the quality of life for all.

Despite claims by animal rights activists, it is undeniable that animal-based research has contributed to significant improvement in the length and quality of our lives. Following are just a few specific cases in which the use of laboratory animals has been a vital component of medical progress.

Indeed, wherever one might stand on the issue, we *all* benefit from the use of laboratory animals in biomedical research!

Innovations in Cancer Treatments

New cancer drugs account for 50–60 percent of the gains we have made in cancer survival rates since 1975. Overall, these medicines have contributed a remarkable 10.7% of the increase in life expectancy at birth in the United States. Until recently, surgery, radiation therapy and chemotherapy were the dominant treatments for cancer. But now, thanks in large part to animal-based research, there is a new molecular and genetic understanding of tumor biology, leading to treatments that set out to more directly kill cancer cells, which are molecularly different from normal cells. Use of this knowledge to design drugs that focus on those abnormalities is called rational drug design, and is seen by many as the currently emerging future reality of cancer treatment—of "kinder and gentler" cancer therapies that only target abnormal cells.

- Breast Cancer—According to the Carol M. Baldwin Breast Cancer Research Fund, "This year, approximately 182,800 women in the United States will be diagnosed with invasive breast cancer, and approximately 40,800 women will die from breast cancer." Her son, actor Alec Baldwin, who serves on the advisory board of the Fund and received PETA's Humanitarian Award in 2005, has broken with PETA over the value of animal research in developing treatments for breast cancer. In March 1998, he told *USA Today*, "One cannot be 'single issue' when it comes to medical research." He's right. Animal research was essential for the development of Herceptin and Tamoxifen, two medicines that have saved the lives of thousands of women and men with breast cancer.

- Childhood Leukemia—Once a virtual death sentence, acute lymphoblastic leukemia (ALL) is the most common of childhood cancers. When St. Jude Children's Research Hospital, founded by actor Danny Thomas, opened in Memphis in 1962, the survival rate was four percent. St. Jude's revolutionized leukemia therapy and today 80 percent of the children survive. Now, scientists are working to develop even more effective and less-toxic drugs through genetic identification of the major subtypes of childhood ALL.

- Chronic Myeloid Leukemia—A discovery that a combined protein caused leukemia in mice led to the development of Gleevec, the first molecularly targeted drug against cancer. It was approved by the FDA in May 2001 for treatment of CML, which affects 5,000–8,000 people a year. It is also used to treat a rare, previously incurable form of stomach cancer known as gastrointestinal stromal tumor (GIST).

- Lung Cancer—Lung cancer is the leading cause of cancer death for both men and women in the United States, killing more people than breast, prostate, colon and pancreas cancers combined. A 2001 report from the National Cancer Institute stressed the dire need for research relying on mouse models of lung cancer and focusing on understanding, preventing, and detecting lung cancer and developing novel targeted therapies for treating the disease.

Advancements in HIV/AIDS Therapies

A cure has not yet been found for HIV/AIDS, but with new therapies HIV has become a chronic disease, and infected persons are living normal lives for many years. Research, including work with animal models, continues to develop new medicines with fewer side effects, as well as to create vaccine candidates that may one day make HIV infection preventable.

- Combination drug therapy—Thanks to the approval in 1995 of protease inhibitors—and further advancements in new medicines and combination therapies in the decade since—the AIDS death rate in the United States has fallen by 70 percent.

- Pediatric AIDS—There are more than 9,000 cases of AIDS in children (diagnosed before age 13) in the United States. There are many more children living with HIV. According to the Elizabeth Glaser Pediatric

AIDS Foundation, about 2.1 million children are living with HIV worldwide, and there are 1,350 AIDS deaths in children every day. Effective anti-viral therapy given to the mother during pregnancy and labor and to the child can reduce transmission to five to eight percent or even less. Scientists are continuing their work with animals to gain a better understanding of mother-to-infant HIV transmission.

Scientists have been able to produce and grow a dopamine-producing cell line and test it in mouse models of Parkinson's disease.

Major Progress in Heart Disease and Stroke Treatment and Prevention

The progress made in reducing death rates from heart disease and stroke is saving the lives of over one million Americans each year.

- Statins—Millions of people take a statin pill once a day to control their high cholesterol and reduce their risk of heart disease. Statins were introduced in 1987. Doctors believe that if all patients at risk took statins according to guidelines, heart disease would no longer be the number one killer of Americans.

- "Clot-busting agents"—In 2003, the American Stroke Association recommended the administration of rt-PA immediately following a stroke. Patients thus treated are more likely to have minimal or even no disability following a stroke.

- Nutrition—Much of what doctors know about the role of the foods we eat in preventing heart disease and high cholesterol comes from animal studies.

Further Innovations

Diabetes. 18.2 million people—6.3 percent of the U.S. population—have diabetes, which is a leading cause of death and disability. Diabetes also affects animals and has been diagnosed in virtually every breed of dog and cat. Several new treatments and medicines, including development of quick-acting and long-acting insulins, islet transplantation for type 1 diabetes, and new drugs to treat type 2 diabetes are helping patients manage their disease. Research involving animal models continues to improve treatments for chronic complications including blindness, kidney disease, heart disease and stroke.

Parkinson's Disease. According to the Michael J. Fox Foundation for Parkinson's Research, "In the past few years, Parkinson's research has advanced to the point that halting disease progression and even preventing Parkinson's are considered realistic goals."

- Stem Cells—One of the most promising avenues of research is stem cell therapy. Scientists have been able to produce and grow a dopamine-producing cell line and test it in mouse models of Parkinson's disease. Now, a second cell line is being developed for testing in laboratory animals that seeks to advance understanding of the process by which dopaminergic neurons are generated.

- Neurotrophic Factors—In animal studies, this family of proteins has revived dormant brain cells, caused them to produce dopamine, and prompted dramatic improvement of symptoms. Human trials are now underway.

Hepatitis C. Just over 20 years ago, the hepatitis C virus was identified. Since then, the first steps have been taken toward treatments that can apply to and help the majority of patients. Approximately 80 percent of people infected with acute hepatitis C virus develop a chronic infection, which can lead to severe liver problems, such as cirrhosis—permanent scarring of the liver. Cirrhosis is the seventh leading cause of death by disease, and kills approximately 27,000 Americans each year. Patients with cirrhosis are at risk for developing liver cancer and, eventually, liver failure. In fact, about five percent of all people with hepatitis C will eventually need a liver transplant as a result of liver cancer or liver failure. The current standard therapy for hepatitis C, with Interferon and Ribavirin, does not work in every patient and can be fraught with troublesome side effects. Researchers are at work now on a new class of therapies, involving protease and polymerase inhibitors, which may ultimately produce a vaccine and/or a cure for hepatitis C.

Animal studies will continue to play a necessary role in neuroscientists' efforts to understand and treat seizure disorders.

Birth Defects. Every three and a half minutes, a baby is born with a birth defect in the United States.

- Folic Acid—Studies with animals determined that folic acid, a B vitamin, helps prevent serious birth defects of the brain and spinal cord when taken before conception and early in pregnancy. Since this discovery, a public education campaign launched in 1992 has prevented thousands of such birth defects.

- Surfactant Therapy—One in eight babies in the United States is born too soon. The lungs in many of these premature children are not fully developed. Surfactant is a detergent-like substance produced in the lungs that aids in breathing. Since surfactant therapy became widespread in the 1980s, infant deaths due to respiratory distress syndrome have dropped by over two-thirds. Research supported by the March of Dimes and others continues to seek new, more effective therapies.

Bioterrorism Medical Countermeasures. Animal research is a key component of work underway to address the threat that terrorists may one day use a biological agent in the United States. Currently, there are vaccine candidates in various stages of development for anthrax, plague, Ebola virus, hantaviruses, botulinum neurotoxins, and nearly a dozen other agents. Research on treatments focuses on the development of new antimicrobials and antitoxins, as well as the screening of existing antimicrobial agents to determine whether they would be effective against organisms that might be used by terrorists.

Animal Studies Continue to Play a Significant Role

Epilepsy. 2.7 million Americans have an active seizure disorder. Doctors estimate that only about half of all people battling epilepsy have their seizures under control and are able to live normal lives. People with epilepsy are counting on biomedical research to improve their well-being. People and animals share many basic brain structures and both are subject to epilepsy. Thus, for the foreseeable future, animal studies will continue to play a necessary role in neuroscientists' efforts to understand and treat seizure disorders.

- New Medicines—In the past decade, nine new medicines for treating epilepsy have become available to patients, and eight treatments are in the pipeline to offer better control of seizures, with fewer side effects.

- Improved Surgical Techniques—Advanced neurosurgical procedures, first developed in animals, are able to help some patients to become seizure-free or decrease the number and severity of their seizures. Vagus nerve stimulation has proven to be a crucial tool in controlling the seizures of other patients.

Spinal Cord Injuries. The Christopher and Dana Reeve Paralysis Foundation notes that amazingly, more research progress has been achieved in the past five years than in the previous fifty. Now that the age-old dogma that the spinal cord could not be repaired has been debunked, scientists feel they are on the threshold of major discoveries that will lead to new treatments. Animal models are used for exploring repair and recovery of the spinal cord. The search for a cure for paralysis could also yield advances in the treatment of other neurological disorders, such as multiple sclerosis, Parkinson's, Alzheimer's, Huntington's and the aftereffects of stroke.

Cystic Fibrosis. Advances in medical treatment have greatly improved the quality of life and life expectancy of children diagnosed with this inherited disease that affects breathing and digestion. While at one time CF almost invariably killed babies, most of those affected now survive to their mid-30s, though some die in childhood and others live to age 40 or beyond. The abnormal gene that causes CF was discovered in 1989. A number of new drugs that aim to prevent or treat infections in those with CF are currently being tested. However, there is still no cure. Research, including the use of animal models, must continue if a cure is to be found.

2

Animal Research Is Unethical and Scientifically Unnecessary

American Anti-Vivisection Society

The American Anti-Vivisection Society (AAVS) is a nonprofit animal advocacy and educational organization dedicated to ending experimentation on animals in research, testing, and education in the United States. AAVS also opposes other forms of cruelty to animals.

It is wrong to treat animals as objects for the purpose of scientific research, and to cause them pain and suffering. It is not possible to use animal outcomes to predict results in humans. The current emphasis on animal "models" in biomedical research should be replaced by more relevant and effective alternatives and by an emphasis on clinical research and attention to preventative measures.

Scientists use animals in biological and medical research more as a matter of tradition, not because animal research has proved particularly successful or better than other modes of experimentation. In fact, animal 'models' have never been validated, and the claim that animals are necessary for biomedical research is unsupported by the scientific literature. Instead, there is growing awareness of the limitations of animal research and its inability to make reliable predictions about human health.

The biomedical research community and its affiliated trade associations routinely attempt to convince the general public, media, and government representatives that the current controversy over the use of animals is a life-and-death contest pitting defenders of human health and scientific advancement against hordes of anti-science, anti-human, emotional, irrational activists. Such a deliberate, simplistic dichotomy is not only false, but ignores the very real and well-documented ethical and scientific problems associated with the use of animal experiments that characterize modern biomedical research, testing, and its associated industries.

The biomedical community would instead be better served by promoting increased funding and research efforts for the development of non-animal models that overcome the pressing ethical and scientific limitations of an increasingly archaic system of animal experimentation.

Ethical Concerns of Using Animals in Research

Animals are living, sentient beings, and animal experimentation by its very nature takes a considerable toll on animal life. In most cases, researchers attempt to minimize the pain and distress experienced by animals in laboratories, but suffering is nonetheless inherent as animals are held in sterile, isolated cages, forced to suffer disease and injury, or euthanised at the end of the study.

Obvious and subtle differences between humans and animals in terms of our physiology, anatomy, and metabolism make it difficult to apply data derived from animal studies to human conditions.

While the majority of scientists are well-intentioned, focused on finding cures for what ails us, some biomedical researchers fail to recognize or appreciate that laboratory animals are not simply machines or little boxes that produce varieties of data. Once consideration of animals is reduced to this level, callousness and insensitivity to the animals' pain, suffering, and basic needs can follow.

Indeed, animals in laboratories are frequently treated as objects that can be manipulated at will, with little value for their lives beyond the cost of purchase. AAVS [American Anti-Vivisection Society], however, believes that animals have the right *not* to be exploited for science, and we should not have to choose between helping humans and harming animals.

Scientific Limitations of Using Animals

In addition to the ethical arguments against using animals in research, animal advocates, as well as many scientists, are increasingly questioning the scientific validity and reliability of animal experimentation. Some of the main limitations of animal research are discussed in detail below:

- Animal studies do not reliably predict human outcomes.

- Nine out of ten drugs that appear promising in animal studies go on to fail in human clinical trials.

- Reliance on animal experimentation can impede and delay discovery.

- Animal studies are flawed by design.

Animal studies do not reliably predict human outcomes. Obvious and subtle differences between humans and animals in terms of our physiology, anatomy, and metabolism make it difficult to apply data derived from animal studies to human conditions. Acetaminophen, for example, is poisonous to cats but is therapeutic in humans; penicillin is toxic in guinea pigs but has been an invaluable tool in human medicine; morphine causes hyper-excitement in cats but has a calming effect in human patients; and oral contraceptives prolong blood-clotting times in dogs but increase a human's risk of developing blood clots. Many more such examples exist. Even within the same species, similar disparities can be found among different sexes, breeds, age and weight ranges, and ethnic backgrounds.

Furthermore, animal 'models' are seldom subject to the same causes, symptoms, or biological mechanisms as their purported human analogues. Indeed, many health problems currently afflicting humans, such as psychopathology, cancer, drug addiction, Alzheimer's, and AIDS, are species-specific.

As a result, accurately translating information from animal studies to human patients can be an exercise in speculation. According to [D.G.] Hackam and [D.A.] Redelmeier (2006), "patients and physicians should remain cautious about extrapolating the findings of prominent animal research to the care of human disease," and even high-quality animal studies will replicate poorly in human clinical research.

Alternatively, drugs and procedures that could be effective in humans may never be developed because they fail in animal studies.

Nine out of ten drugs that appear promising in animal studies go on to fail in human clinical trials. Indeed, because of the inherent differences between animals and humans, drugs and procedures that work in animals often end up failing in humans. According to Health and Human Services Secretary Mike Leavitt, "nine out of ten experimental drugs fail in clinical studies because we cannot accurately predict how they will behave in people based on laboratory and animal studies."

A significant amount of time and money, not to mention animal lives, is squandered in the process. Pfizer, for example, reported in 2004 that it had wasted more than $2 billion over the past decade on drugs that "failed in advanced human testing or, in a few instances, were forced off the market, because of liver toxicity problems."

In fact, there have been numerous reports recently of approved drugs causing serious and unexpected health problems, leading the Food and Drug Administration (FDA) to remove the products from the market or require black box warnings on their labels. The FDA has reported that "adverse events associated with drugs are the single leading contributor to preventable patient injury, and may cost the lives of up to 100,000 Americans, account for more than 3 million hospital admissions, and increase the nation's hospitalization bill by up to $17 billion each year." The agency estimates that drug-related injuries outside the hospital add $76.6 billion to health care costs.

Reliance on animal experimentation can impede and delay discovery. Alternatively, drugs and procedures that could be effective in humans may never be developed because they fail in animal studies. It is difficult to know how frequently this occurs, since drugs that fail in animals are rarely tested in humans. However, there have been some notable cases. Lipitor, for example, Pfizer's blockbuster drug for reducing cholesterol, did not seem promising in early animal experiments. A research scientist, however, requested that the drug be tested in a small group of healthy human volunteers, and it was only then that its effectiveness was demonstrated.

In many instances, medical discoveries are delayed as researchers vainly waste time, money, effort, and animal lives trying to create an animal model of a human disease. A classic example is the discovery that smoking significantly increases the risk of lung cancer. The finding was first reported in 1954 on the basis of an epidemiological study. The report was dismissed, however, because lung cancer due to inhalation of cigarette smoke could not be induced in animal models, and it wasn't until 30 years later that the U.S. Surgeon General finally issued the warning on cigarettes.

Another noteworthy example concerns the development of the polio vaccine. Researchers spent decades infecting nonhuman primates with the disease and conducting other animal experiments, but failed to produce a vaccine. The key event which led directly to the vaccine and a Nobel Prize occurred when researchers grew the virus in human cell cultures *in vitro*.

In animal research, as with slot machines, if you pull the traditional levers enough times, a winner eventually appears.

Animal studies are flawed by design. In addition to the fact that animals make poor surrogates for humans, the design of animal experiments is often inherently flawed, making it that much more unlikely that results obtained from such studies will be useful. Researchers from the Vanderbilt University Medical Center [S.M. Williams, J.L. Haines, and J.H. Moore] described some of the problems with animal 'models' in their 2004 article: "... [T]he design of animal studies automatically controls many variables that can confound human studies"; "... [T]he phenotypes studied in animals are not truly identical to human disease but are limited representations of them"; and "In most cases, animal studies do not assess the role of naturally occurring variation and its effects on phenotypes."

Furthermore, in their effort to secure research funds, expand the territorial boundaries and influence of their laboratories, or simply maintain their employment, it is a common practice for biomedical researchers to generate an endless series of experiments by devising minor variations on a common theme, redefining previous work, subdividing one problem into multiple parts, or manipulating new technology and equipment to answer old or irrelevant questions. Such practices are endemic in such fields as experimental psychology, substance abuse/addiction, and most of the neuroscience and transplantation protocols, yet by their very design do little to improve human or animal lives.

Promise of Alternatives

In animal research, as with slot machines, if you pull the traditional levers enough times, a winner eventually appears. However, animal research, in addition to being ethically challenged, is also highly flawed and severely limited, and as such, the majority of such research has failed to translate into improvements in human health.

Despite the problems with animal research, there continues to be an over-reliance on questionable animal 'models,' and there has been [according to the FDA] "an unprecedented increase in funding for biomedical research" over the years, without much success.

If the goal of biomedical experimentation is the understanding and treatment of human clinical concerns, then the current emphasis on animal 'models,' constructed under multiple artificial conditions, should be replaced by more relevant alternatives and a return to an emphasis on clinical research and public health attention to preventative measures.

Even in areas that have come to rely on vivisection, ending animal experimentation would not halt research because experience shows that scientists quickly devise new techniques to achieve their objectives. Epidemiology, cell culture experiments, and human clinical studies, as well as recent advances in *in silico* biology (computational modeling), are all better suited to efficiently and safely uncovering the cause of a disease and its treatment than is animal experimentation.

3

Opinion Has Limited the Use of Stray Dogs and Cats in Scientific Research

National Research Council Committee on Scientific and Human Issues in the Use of Random Source Dogs and Cats in Research

The National Research Council Committee on Scientific and Human Issues in the Use of Random Source Dogs and Cats in Research was formed in response to a request by Congress. Its charge was to critically examine the general desirability and necessity of using random source dogs and cats in National Institutes of Health-funded research, and the specific necessity of using dogs and cats from certain types of animal dealers for such research.

While the majority of Americans are in favor of the use of animals for research on serious medical problems, support has been eroding in recent years. Americans are less supportive of the use of dogs, cats, and other "companion" animals than they are of the use of animals, such as mice, that are specially bred for research. Lack of public support for the use of dogs and cats in research has resulted in decreased use of these animals, and in stronger efforts by the US Department of Agriculture to regulate certain animal dealers known as Class B dealers, a group that includes brokers, operators of auctions, and dealers that collect animals from shelters and individual owners.

Dogs and cats occupy a particularly important place in American society in their roles as companion, work, and hobby animals. In addition, they serve as important animal models for research that has advanced both human and animal health. This multifaceted relationship with humans has fostered an uneasy tension between general society and the scientific community, and this tension has intensified as the stature of pet dogs and cats has risen in many households to that of family member. The specter of lost or stolen pets being used for research has evolved from a galvanizing concern into increasing resistance to the use of any former pet for research. Over the years the public's concern about the welfare of research animals, and dogs and cats in particular, has been instrumental in the development of laws, guidelines, and policies that affect research with all types of animals.

Several sources have suggested that 6–12% of the dog population entered shelters in the 1990s and that approximately 50–55% were euthanized.

It is thus not possible to accurately assess the desirability and necessity of using random source dogs and cats, and in particular those from Class B dealers [Class B dealers include brokers, operators of auctions, and "bunchers" who collect dogs, cats, and other regulated animals from random sources], for research without taking into account public perceptions, the impact of the animal protection movement both on public attitudes and on the availability of these animals for research, changing trends in the use of animal models for research, and responses of the scientific community to all of these factors. The evolution of laws, policies, and guidelines regarding the use of dogs and cats in research has been an accurate barometer of these changing trends.

In particular, in 2007 the Senate considered the Pet Safety and Protection Act, which became the impetus for Congress to charge the National Institutes of Health (NIH) to deter-mine the humane and scientific issues associated with the use of random source dogs and cats in research. Consequently, NIH asked the National Academies to assemble a committee of experts to address the . . . use of random source animals, and animals from Class B dealers in NIH-funded research.

Public Perceptions of Dogs and Cats and of Their Use in Research

The public's perception of their pets, and of animals in gen-eral, has been one of the main driving forces behind the legis-lation that created and refined the Animal Welfare Act (AWA). It is estimated that nearly half of all U.S. households have at least one dog or cat, with a total population of 72 million dogs and nearly 82 million cats. In a survey conducted by the American Animal Hospital Association, approximately 94% of owners attributed human personality traits to their pets and said they would risk their lives for their pet. Indeed, in urban disasters, pet owners risk their lives (and those of rescue workers) when they fail to evacuate or attempt to reenter an unsafe building or area to save a pet. In addition, pet owners spend over $11 billion per year on veterinary care, and the pet products industry contributes over $50 billion to the U.S. economy, with the exponential growth of pet super-stores, play parks, day care centers, and training centers.

Assessments of pet ownership and the state of affairs of dogs and cats in the U.S. must take into account the plight of homeless animals. However, it is impossible to provide a cur-rent or accurate estimate of the numbers of animals that enter shelters or are euthanized because there is no federal require-ment to gather or release such data, shelters may obscure or refuse to release data to avoid negative publicity, and there is no reliable public list of shelters. Furthermore, although "shel-ter" or "pound" is defined in this report as a "facility that op-erates as a pound or shelter (e.g., a humane society or other organization established for the purpose of caring for animals), under contract with a state, county, or city, and that releases animals on a voluntary basis" the shelter data provided in this chapter may include statistics from other facilities commonly referred to as shelters. In the absence of accurate statistics, the estimated number of animals euthanized in shelters was 4.5 and 4.6 million in 1999 and 2000, respectively.

The inflow of animals into shelters varies considerably by area of the country and even among shelters within an area. Several sources have suggested that 6–12% of the dog population entered shelters in the 1990s and that approximately 50–55% were euthanized (representing 4% of the total dog population), and that 5–8% of the estimated population of owned cats entered shelters and 65–80% of those (or roughly 3–6% of the total population of owned cats) were euthanized.

Although those percentages have likely changed since the 1990s, one might be able to make a rough estimate of the shelter intake numbers for any given year by taking AVMA [American Veterinary Medical Association] demographic numbers of owned dogs and cats and multiplying them by the percentages above. According to the 2007 AVMA *U.S. Pet Ownership and Demographics Sourcebook*, the population of owned dogs in 2006 in the U.S. was 72 million and the number of owned cats was 81.7 million. Those figures suggest that 4.3 to 8.6 million dogs and 4.1 to 6.5 million cats may have entered shelters, and as many as 7 million animals may have been euthanized.

Consideration of public perceptions was important to the Committee's analysis, and such information is generally derived from surveys and other sources. Although there is a risk of bias in polls and surveys, it appears that a majority of the American public is generally supportive of the use of animals in biomedical research but that the proportion has declined significantly over the last several decades, from about 85% in 1950 to 50–60% in the late 1990s and early 2000s. The reasons for this decline are unknown, although they appear to reflect changes in public attitudes to a wide variety of animal-related issues over the same period. In 2008 the Foundation for Biomedical Research (FBR) commissioned Zogby International to conduct a nationwide telephone survey. The survey revealed that although a majority of those polled supported the use of animals for medical and scientific research, they were much less supportive than those polled in 2004. Other survey findings suggest that public support for animal research is influenced by the perceived importance of the medical problem being researched and the type of animal used. The use of animals (of any type) to study relatively serious medical problems (e.g., cancer, heart disease, diabetes) tends to garner more support than their use for studying relatively minor problems (e.g., allergies), while research involving the use of dogs and cats receives considerably less support than that involving the use of rodents. These findings illustrate the higher value that the American public places on dogs, cats, and other companion animals.

The iconic species that continue to capture public sympathy are the dog, cat, horse, and nonhuman primate.

The Animal Protection Movement

The animal protection movement has had a profound impact on public attitudes toward the use of animals in research and on the evolution of laws, policies, and voluntary compliance by the scientific community.

[J.] Jasper and [D.] Nelkin (1992) defined three types of animal protectionists: welfarists, pragmatists, and fundamentalists. Welfarists accept most current uses of animals, but seek to minimize their suffering. Pragmatists and fundamentalists are motivated to invoke fundamental changes in the use of animals by humans, but pragmatists seek to reduce animal use through legal actions, political protests, and negotiation whereas fundamentalists demand the abolition of all exploitation of animals, on the grounds that animals have inherent, inviolable rights. Clearly, it is impossible to classify every individual into one of these categories but this system may be a useful way to understand individual motivations.

Since the beginning of the animal protection movement in Europe in the early 1800s up through the present, the iconic species that continue to capture public sympathy are the dog, cat, horse, and nonhuman primate. The U.S. animal protection community is large and varied—in 1994, there were over 400 animal advocacy groups, with a combined membership of more than 10 million, and these figures have likely grown substantially since then. These groups include organizations such as the Animal Welfare Institute (AWI), which focuses on the welfare of research animals and has published graphic documentation of animal dealer abuse; the Humane Society of the United States (HSUS), which seeks to eliminate animal-based research that is harmful to animals; and People for the Ethical Treatment of Animals (PETA), which seeks to eliminate all exploitive uses (research, food, fiber, and entertainment) of animals by humans. At the extreme end of the spectrum of the animal rights organizations is the Animal Liberation Front (ALF), which uses acts of intimidation, terrorism, and violence to disrupt the scientific enterprise as well as to "liberate" animals from use in sports, textiles, research, and agriculture. The actions of organizations such as the ALF have been designated as terrorism and resulted in passage of the Animal Enterprise Terrorism Act (S. 3880), introduced by Congressman Thomas Petri (R-WI) and signed into law on November 27, 2006.

Evolution of Animal Care Oversight Within the Scientific Community

The scientific community has had a long and contentious relationship with animal protection groups since the 1800s. In the past, the research community could be described as maintaining a somewhat imperious attitude toward the public, with overconfidence that what it was doing was right. Over the years, however, the scientific community has evolved the view that healthy and well-maintained animals are beneficial to and necessary for quality research and, indeed, has promulgated voluntary compliance beyond that which is mandated by law.

Since the early 1950s—well before the 1966 Laboratory Animal Welfare Act and the 1985 Research Animals Congressional Mandate—the biomedical research community has engaged in organized efforts to improve and ensure the humane care and use of animals in research. Prominent nongovernmental scientific organizations include the National Research Council's Institute for Laboratory Animal Research (ILAR); the American College of Laboratory Animal Medicine (ACLAM), established in 1957 to advance the humane care and responsible use of laboratory animals through certification of veterinary specialists, professional development, education, and research; and the Association for Assessment and Accreditation of Laboratory Animal Care International (AAALAC International).

Since its creation in 1953, ILAR has played a critical role in developing and publishing numerous science-based guidelines on issues involving animals in research settings. The most important of the ILAR reports is the *Guide for the Care and Use of Laboratory Animals*, published under the 1963 title 3 years before the Laboratory Animal Welfare Act became law and is periodically updated. Since 1965, compliance with the *Guide* has been the AAALAC International standard for institutions seeking accreditation (in 2009, 770 institutions in 31 countries reported having been accredited), and . . . the *Guide* has been incorporated by reference in federal guidelines for government-funded research.

The National Institutes of Health has also been at the forefront of efforts to improve both scientific research and laboratory animal care. In 1961 NIH funded a contract to the

Animal Care Panel (now AALAS) to "determine and establish a professional standard for laboratory animal care and facilities." The Panel appointed a Committee on Ethical Considerations in the Care of Laboratory Animals and a Professional Standards Committee to evaluate laboratory animal care and use, and their efforts, in collaboration with ILAR, resulted in the 1963 publication of the *Guide for Laboratory Animal Facilities and Care*. NIH also led the way in development of the *Public Health Service (PHS) Policy* that applies to most federally funded animal research. The *PHS Policy* requires that institutions eligible for PHS funding use the *Guide* "as a basis for the development and implementation of an institutional program for activities involving animals," and the *U.S. Government Principles* similarly refer to the *Guide*.

Despite improvements in the biomedical research community, the use of random source dogs and cats, and animals from Class B dealers, remains a divisive and publicly visible issue.

Although the scientific community has come to embrace changes leading to the improved health and welfare of animal research subjects, at the same time the perception within the research community is that it has been under siege. Attacks on and intimidation of scientists by extremist organizations have increased dramatically in recent years. Furthermore, as animal protection groups have pushed for greater regulation of animal research, the cost of regulatory compliance in terms of dollars and time has become an increasing burden on biomedical research, even though it is not clear that the increased regulatory oversight directly benefits the health and welfare of the animals. When regulations do not improve animal health and well-being, they are no more than regulatory burden. An earlier report noted the diminishing availability of random source animals nearly 20 years ago. The research community has attempted to push back against these trends through national science advocacy groups such as the FBR, the National Association for Biomedical Research (NABR), and Americans for Medical Progress (AMP), all of which work to educate the public about the importance of animals in research.

The Impact of the Animal Protection Movement

Despite improvements in the biomedical research community, the use of random source dogs and cats, and animals from Class B dealers, remains a divisive and publicly visible issue. The consequences of the animal protection movement and public opinion are (1) reduced access to random source dogs and cats from pounds and shelters, (2) increased USDA efforts to inspect and enforce the AWA in regards to Class B dealers, and (3) pressure on research institutions to use purpose-bred animals from Class A dealers [licensed commercial breeders], to explore alternative sources of animals (e.g., donation programs, direct acquisition), to use non-animal models, and to use less iconic species (e.g., pigs, small ruminants, in addition to rats, mice, and other rodents). Other causes of the declining use of dogs and cats in research include reduced research funding, changing NIH program priorities, increased regulatory burden, and greater availability of other models. Animal protection activity is one of several factors that have contributed to these trends.

4

Use of Chimpanzees in Scientific Research Should Be Banned

Marc Bekoff

Marc Bekoff is a former professor of ecology and evolutionary biology at the University of Colorado, Boulder. He is the cofounder, with Jane Goodall, of Ethologists for the Ethical Treatment of Animals. His books include the Encyclopedia of Animal Rights and Animal Welfare, *the* Encyclopedia of Human-Animal Relationships, The Emotional Lives of Animals, *and* The Animal Manifesto: Six Reasons for Increasing Our Compassion Footprint.

A recent report by the Institute of Medicine examined the necessity of using chimpanzees in biomedical research. The report did not identify any current research field in which the use of chimpanzees was definitely necessary. However, the report did not ban chimpanzee research in the future. This conclusion fails to take into account the moral significance of the emotional and physical suffering of the animals. Most advanced nations have banned the use of chimpanzees in medical research, and the United States should do so as well.

Few fields of science are more dogged by controversy than experimentation on chimpanzees. On the one hand, chimpanzees are our closest living relatives, which makes them potentially superior to all other species in predicting human responses to new drugs or other clinical interventions. On the other hand, their advanced psychological and social characteristics also increase their risks of suffering, when subjected to confinement, social disruption, and participation in invasive and potentially harmful research. Furthermore, severe abuse during research projects has also been documented in major research facilities.

Accordingly, invasive chimpanzee research is increasingly attracting the concern of scientists, philosophers, legislators and the public and chimpanzees are winning some small victories. On December 15, 2011, this resulted in the release of an expert report by the Institute of Medicine (IOM) called "Chimpanzees in Biomedical and Behavioral Research: Assessing the Necessity." This report failed to identify any current research field in which such research is definitely necessary. Yet it stopped short of recommending an outright ban, concluding that, "a new, emerging, or reemerging disease or disorder may present challenges to treatment, prevention, and/or control that defy non-chimpanzee models and technologies and thus may require their future use." Thus, some researchers such as Dr. John VandeBerg, Director of the Texas Biomedical Research Institute in San Antonio, Texas, sickeningly view chimpanzees as books on a shelf in a library waiting to be used if they're needed.

The ethical foundations for conducting [biomedical] research [on chimpanzees] are deeply questionable.

The Horrific Costs to Chimpanzees

In coming to this conclusion, however, the IOM appeared to give little consideration to the many, varying, and complex animal welfare problems accruing from such research. Yet these may be profound. In his recent book *The Costs and Ben-*

efits of Animal Experiments, Australian veterinarian Andrew Knight examined in detail the costs incurred by chimpanzees and other animals subjected to biomedical research, and the human benefits that result from it. Recent studies have established beyond any doubt that the effects of all sorts of research on laboratory animals, especially long term, can be severe. Chimpanzees recently retired from U. S. laboratories exhibit gross stereotypes (repetitive, apparently purposeless behaviors) indicating psychological distress that is both profound and chronic. Other behavioral abnormalities include self-mutilation, inappropriate aggression, fear, withdrawal, and mood and anxiety disorders including post-traumatic stress disorder (PTSD).

The implications of what we're learning about the incredible suffering of chimpanzees and other animals who are used in invasive research are medically and morally profound. As Knight states, "It is increasingly acknowledged that such abnormal behaviours resemble symptoms associated with human psychiatric disorders such as depression, anxiety disorders, eating disorders, and post-traumatic stress disorder, and that pharmacological treatment modalities similar to those applied to human patients may be appropriate, and, indeed, morally compelled, for severely disturbed animal patients. . . . Long-term therapeutic combination with positive reinforcement training, environmental enrichment, and social and environmental modification may be necessary in severe cases."

Differing Treatment Standards

The ethical foundations for conducting such research are deeply questionable. To illustrate this point, Knight asks us to consider an analogous legal scenario:

"Although these highly sentient creatures are innocent of causing any human grievance, including the serious diseases we attempt to induce in them, we sometimes subject chimpanzees to conditions that would cause widespread outrage if used to punish the most heinous of human criminals—for years on end, and, in some cases, for decades. . . . In contrast, human criminals are not normally punished until proven guilty beyond reasonable doubt. The application of such differing treatment standards to humans and chimpanzees reveals a lack of 'humanity' paradoxically less characteristic of chimpanzees, than of ourselves."

Not a year seems to pass without important new discoveries about hitherto unsuspected animal cognitive abilities and emotional capacities that remind us how much we still have to learn about other species.

The Bases for Moral Consideration

Exactly what morally profound differences between chimpanzees and humans justify such markedly differing treatment standards? Their highly evolved psychological and social characteristics create a strong ethical basis for respecting at least their most basic and essential needs, such as their interests in avoiding being kept in small cages in captivity, pain, suffering and death. Those who would deny such consideration to chimpanzees and other animals usually try to claim the existence in humans of some morally relevant characteristic(s) supposedly absent in other species, such as intelligence, language, or tool-use. Interestingly, however, they nevertheless usually extend such consideration to very young, old, injured, or ill humans, who also lack such abilities to various degrees.

It is absolutely right that we should continue to value such people as partially conscious or partially self-conscious beings, with unique personalities, and accordingly grant them human rights. However, it is logically consistent to consider animals who possess human-like psychological characteristics, such as consciousness and self-consciousness, the capacity to experience emotional states, and the possession of significant cognitive abilities, as non-human persons, who should also be granted certain fundamental rights concordant with those granted to humans. After all, as Knight puts it, "no matter how equal all humans actually are, all are considered equal in dignity and rights."

It is also worth considering that not a year seems to pass without important new discoveries about hitherto unsuspected animal cognitive abilities and emotional capacities, that remind us how much we still have to learn about other species. While significant doubt remains, it seems fair to extend to animals the benefit of that doubt because current data show clearly that much of what we thought to be true of other animals actually is.

Money, Self-Interest, and False Assumptions

Contrary to such ethical considerations, the U. S. remains heavily involved in invasive chimpanzee research. As of May 2011, some 937 chimpanzees remained incarcerated within U. S. laboratories. The lifetime cost of supporting 650 federally funded chimpanzees was estimated at $325 million in 2007. Virtually every other country, with the possible exception of Gabon, whose status is unclear, has long since terminated such research. Why, then, does the U. S. persist?

Unfortunately, the answers center on money, self-interest, and false assumptions. Researchers whose grants and careers depend on such research frequently claim it has been of crucial importance in combatting serious human diseases, although rigorous supporting evidence is rarely, if ever, forthcoming. In his book Knight thoroughly tests such claims, by surveying the published scientific literature to determine the proportion of invasive chimpanzee studies that actually contribute to human medical advancements.

He shows that the majority of such studies actually remain un-cited by subsequent scientific papers in any field of research, thereby contributing little to the advancement of biomedical knowledge. Only some 15% of chimpanzee studies are cited by papers describing medical interventions potentially effective in humans. However, detailed examination of such medical papers reveal that in vitro (cell-based) studies, human clinical and population studies, molecular methods and tests, and genome studies, are by far the most important sources of knowledge. Most chimpanzee studies are, at best, of peripheral importance, and none of those studied by Knight and his colleagues made an essential contribution, or, in most cases, a significant contribution of any kind, to the development of the medical methods studied. . . .

Other Laboratory Species

What about other species used in laboratories? As Knight puts it, "given that other animal models are even less likely to be generally predictive of human outcomes than chimpanzees . . . by extrapolation, our current reliance on animal models of humans must be questioned in all fields of clinically oriented biomedical research and toxicity testing."

The wealth of data Knight provides confirms this conclusion. He draws on more than a decade of research and over 500 scientific publications to rigorously test common assumptions about animal experimentation. He offers revealing insights into the true contributions of such research to human healthcare, as well as the nature, severity and prevalence of the impacts experienced by laboratory animals. He comprehensively reviews animal use within life and health sciences education, as well as alternative research and educational strategies. This has allowed him to provide, in polished style, one of the most definitive answers yet published to a question with implications for animal ethics, biomedical research, and society at large, namely, "Is animal experimentation ethically justifiable?" And, the answer is a resounding "no".

5

Rats and Mice Are Important for Cancer Research

Guy Mulder

Guy Mulder is the attending veterinarian with Charles River, a company that breeds and sells animals used for biomedical research.

Mice models—mice that have been specially bred for certain traits that are desirable for research—have played an important role in cancer research, and will continue to do so in the future. Recently, attention has turned to the development of rat models. The greater size of rats allows them to tolerate larger drug doses, and also to tolerate the development of larger tumors, as part of a research study. Whether using mice or rats, cancer researchers seek to further their understanding of the disease and take steps toward a cure.

According to the American Cancer Association, more than 1.5 million new cases of cancer were diagnosed in 2010 in the United States alone. More than half a million people succumbed to the disease last year, making it the nation's second deadliest disease.

It isn't necessary to know the exact statistics to understand that cancer is a major concern for both the medical community and lay population. For this reason, the pharmaceutical industry continues to focus resources on discovering compounds for creating effective treatments for this prevalent and still mysterious disease. One of the industry's most valuable in vivo tools [tools for conducting research in a living organism] in that quest is the rodent model.

Mouse Models in Cancer Research

The rodent model has been used in oncology research for several decades. Historically, the mouse has been a model of choice for the battery of tests that compounds must undergo to determine efficacy and safety of cancer therapy candidates. Mice, above all other mammalian species, have proven useful in oncology research because of their small size, ease of rearing, and ability to be produced commercially with specific research-valuable traits.

The biomedical research community offers a wide variety of immunodeficient mouse models—models whose immune systems are compromised and allow acceptance and growth of a wide range of xenografts. Each immunodeficient mouse model has its own unique characteristics that have developed either through spontaneously arising mutation or genetic engineering.

In recent years, advances in genetic engineering have allowed the research community to customize mice with specific immunologic deficits that are useful in cancer research without waiting for spontaneous mutations to arise.

Among mice with spontaneous mutation-derived immunodeficiencies—in which an immunodeficiency occurred naturally and then was carefully bred to create a permanent line— the most popular model is the athymic "nude" mouse. Nude mice fail to develop thymus-derived T cells, and consequently will accept a wide range of murine [relating to the rodent family muridae] and xenogenic [involving cells of a different species] tumor transplants. Because the nude mutation blocks normal epithelial development, the mutation also presents with a characteristic hairless phenotype. The lack of hair also makes for a more efficient model since researchers do not have to shave the animal in order to accurately measure subcutaneous tumor growth.

Another commonly-used mouse model carrying a spontaneous mutation is the SCID mouse (severe combined immune deficiency). The SCID mouse lacks both T and B cell lineages. Like the nude mouse, the model is useful in solid tumor biology and related therapeutic development.

In addition to these two classic single-mutation models, numerous additional immunodeficient models have been produced through backcrossing (e.g., transferring a specific trait between two established mouse models). . . .

In recent years, advances in genetic engineering have allowed the research community to customize mice with specific immunologic deficits that are useful in cancer research without waiting for spontaneous mutations to arise. . . .

Rat Models in Cancer Research

Recently, rat models have found themselves in the conversation with regard to in vivo rodent cancer research. Theoretically, rats may provide benefits over the mouse in oncology research because they are larger and, as a result, they allow for prolonged dosing and increased tumor size development compared to mice. Currently, the use of rats in oncology has been hampered by the relative paucity of available models, particularly immunodeficient rat models for use with xenographs. The most common commercially available immunodeficient rat model is the nude rat. Similar to the nude mouse, the rat model is deficient in thymus-derived T cells and its use is similar to the mouse model.

If rats are to play a larger role in the future of oncology research, it will more than likely result from advances in genetic engineering and the ability to create rat knockout models lacking specific genes associated with immune deficiency or tumor development. This activity has already begun, with researchers utilizing genetic engineering to create rat knockout models deficient in several tumor suppressor genes.

Another good example of this type of rat model is the p53 model that is currently on the market. Tumor protein 53 is a well-characterized tumor suppressor that is involved in cell cycle control, apoptosis, angiogenesis, carcinogenesis, senescence, DNA repair, and changes in metabolism. The p53 rat develops a wide variety of malignant tumors, including sarcomas and lymphomas, making it useful for oncology research.

Of course, the type of model chosen for cancer research—rat, mouse, spontaneous mutation, genetically engineered, T cell deficient, or B cell deficient—completely depends on the nature of the research. Like every other facet of drug discovery and development, model choice and utilization is a complicated process that must be tailored to the goals, needs, and limits of the research.

Whether the future of oncology research lies with classic mice or genetically engineered rats, we can anticipate an increase in the number of available models for cancer research, with every refinement further increasing our understanding of the disease and, hopefully, an eventual cure.

6

New Technologies Could Eliminate the Need for Animal Experimentation

Andrew Rowan

Andrew Rowan is the chief executive officer of Humane Society International (HSI) and chief scientific officer of the Humane Society of the United States (HSUS).

Recent technological advances have greatly reduced the need for animal testing. Given the current rate of technological advance, it is possible that by 2050 researchers will be able to answer important questions about the functioning of healthy and diseased human tissues without subjecting animals to harmful procedures.

The US National Academy of Sciences [NAS] released a report in 2007 envisioning a future in which animals would largely disappear from toxicity testing programs. The report, drafted by a panel of experts, proposed that toxicity induced by drugs, food additives, pesticides, and other chemicals be assessed not by observing overt clinical signs in animals but by monitoring perturbations to biological pathways in cultured human cells. Sophisticated bioinformatic technologies could then provide risk predictions that overcome the limitations of animal-based methods, such as low throughput and the questionable relevance of animal results to human physiology. Initially, the report was greeted with skepticism, but that skepticism is giving way to guarded excitement.

In response to the NAS report, the Environmental Protection Agency [EPA], the National Institutes of Health [NIH], the National Toxicology Program [NTP], and the US Food and Drug Administration [FDA] are cooperating to develop new technologies to modernize chemical testing. Former NIH director Elias Zerhouni characterized this effort as the beginning of the end of animal testing.

The movement away from animal experimentation is already underway. Since the mid-seventies, the use of animals in experimentation has fallen by around 50 percent.

A Fraction of the Time, a Fraction of the Cost

We at The Humane Society of the United States and Humane Society International helped establish a consortium in 2009 to promote the need for a coordinated international program of research and development (akin to the Human Genome Project) to implement the NAS vision. We believe that within the next decade or so, we will reach a point where safety testing and risk evaluation of chemicals will be conducted in a fraction of the time, at a fraction of the cost, and with greater predictive relevance for human and environmental safety compared to current, cumbersome animal-based approaches. The initiative has already attracted the attention of many industry partners, including Dow, DuPont, ExxonMobil, Johnson & Johnson, L'Oreal, Procter & Gamble, and Unilever.

Deepwater Horizon: Testing Could Have Taken Years

The advantages of nonanimal testing methods were illustrated in connection with the recent Gulf of Mexico oil spill. Shortly after the Deepwater Horizon rig began spewing billions of gallons of oil into the Gulf, US political leaders asked the EPA to determine the relative safety of eight different commercially available oil dispersants. Within 6 weeks, the agency tested the eight substances in a number of high-throughput assays that probed a variety of biological pathways, including endocrine disruption and cytotoxicity, and produced a report identifying the toxicity profiles of the dispersants (fortunately, the dispersant being most widely used at the time compared favorably to the others). If these studies had been conducted in animals, the testing and reporting would have taken years, and would likely have produced results no more conclusive than those obtained from the cell systems in a matter of weeks.

For the moment, regulators are reluctant to rely solely on tests based on cell and tissue systems, but as high-throughput systems data become better understood, the speed and cost advantages of these systems will inevitably drive researchers away from whole-animal studies. Current NIH director Francis Collins was an early champion of modernizing toxicity testing, and is now seeking to do the same in efficacy testing. In a recent perspective piece published this past July in *Science Translational Medicine*, Collins characterized the use of animals in developing new therapies as "time consuming" and "costly," adding that such tests "may not accurately predict efficacy in humans." He continued, "With earlier and more rigorous target validation in human tissues, it may be justifiable to skip the animal model assessment of efficacy altogether."

The End in Sight

Indeed, the movement away from animal experimentation is already underway. Since the mid-seventies, the use of animals in experimentation has fallen by around 50 percent. The number of animals held in laboratories of universities and research institutes declined dramatically until around the mid-1990s and then began to climb again as facilities began producing and maintaining genetically modified mouse strains. However, data from Great Britain indicate that the actual use of mice (by far the most-used laboratory species) for research projects has plateaued in the last decade despite a large increase in the size of breeding colonies.

This overall decline in animal use can be attributed to the advent of novel technologies such as improved cell-culture systems and microanalytic techniques; more sophisticated model systems; improved understanding of signaling and metabolic pathways; and a host of other new methods that allow scientists to answer important questions about the functioning of healthy and diseased tissues without subjecting whole animals to harmful procedures. With a 50 percent decline in animal research since 1975, we are roughly at the halfway point towards the complete elimination of animal research. Thus, we argue that, by 2050, we might finally see the last of animal use in the laboratory, particularly if all stakeholders put their minds to it.

7

Research Institutions Must Make the Replacement of Animals a Priority

Physicians Committee for Responsible Medicine

Physicians Committee for Responsible Medicine is a nonprofit organization headquartered in Washington, DC. It advocates for preventive medicine and higher ethical standards in medical research.

Animals used in medical research are frequently subjected to emotional stress, physical pain, and suffering. Scientists and institutions using animals for medical research and education should explore and implement nonanimal methods to the fullest extent possible, with the recognition that in some cases the practical challenges of developing nonanimal methods will not be overcome.

The primary purpose of medical research is to promote human health, and the most direct research methods focus on the study of human populations, individuals, and tissues. Animal research has been used as an alternative method when the study of humans is deemed impractical or unethical, or when animal biology is of primary interest. Animals are frequently used in biological and medical research, in the testing of drugs and commercial products, and in educational exercises in the sciences. While the number of animals used in the United States is not known, estimates range into several tens of millions annually.

Ethical concerns are raised by the use of animals in experimental studies, particularly when they are subjected to painful procedures or toxic exposures. These concerns are accentuated by studies showing marked stress responses in animals undergoing common laboratory procedures. For example, routine handling, venipuncture, and gavage (the administration of test compounds through an oral tube) elicit striking elevations in pulse, blood pressure, and steroid hormone release that can persist for an hour or more after the event. Similarly, routine features of the laboratory environment—isolation, confinement, social disruption, noise, and restrictions on physical movement—have been shown to be noxious for animals. Together, these bodies of evidence indicate that even experiments that appear to be minimally invasive can be highly stressful for the animal subjects, and this finding applies to commonly used rodent species as well as larger and less frequently used animals. Stress effects are relevant to humane concerns as well as to the interpretation of scientific findings. Research on immune function, endocrine and cardiovascular disorders, neoplasms, developmental defects, and psychological phenomena are particularly vulnerable to stress effects.

It is incumbent on scientists and institutions using animals for research, testing, or educational purposes to actively investigate and implement alternatives.

Promoting Nonanimal Methods

Ethical concerns have propelled the exploration of methods that replace animal use. However, such methods may also have scientific advantages related to cost or applicability to human disease. For example, toxicologists seeking more efficient methods have turned to cellular screening tests for many applications and have sometimes realized substantial savings in the process. Trauma training, once conducted almost universally using animals, is now commonly taught with simulators that are cheaper and are designed to more closely mimic critical aspects of patient care.

In August 2007, the US National Research Council published *Toxicity Testing in the 21st Century: A Vision and a Strategy*, which described limitations of animal-based toxicology tests and proposed a new focus on nonanimal methods that may present potential advantages over animal tests. In January 2008, the Environmental Protection Agency and the National Institutes of Health's National Toxicology Program and Chemical Genomics Center signed a Memorandum of Understanding pledging joint funding and research for the replacement of animals in toxicology testing with nonanimal methods. Both documents support the concept that replacement of animal-based methods in toxicology promises practical benefits, aside from humane advances.

It is incumbent on scientists and institutions using animals for research, testing, or educational purposes to actively investigate and implement alternatives. The federal Animal Welfare Act regulations require that research personnel be trained in methods of searching for alternatives to animal use, and the NIH *Guide for the Care and Use of Laboratory Animals* encourages efforts to develop and use scientifically valid alternatives to animal research. There are three broad scenarios for doing so:

1. In some cases, alternatives are readily available. For example, nonanimal methods in medical education have already been implemented for a wide variety of applications at many medical schools, but are not yet in use at all institutions.

2. In other cases, nonanimal methods may not be apparent. In such cases, development of suitable alternative means

should be a high priority. For example, many laboratories produce monoclonal antibodies for research or diagnostic purposes by placing antibody-producing cells in the abdomen of animals, often causing significant pain and distress as the cells produce large amounts of fluid (ascites). While antibodies can also be produced by cellular techniques, there are major technical challenges in so doing for some cell lines.

Pharmaceutical testing presents challenges for the replacement of animal tests. While animal tests leave much to be desired as means of identifying drug-related risks, no alternative test methods are yet acceptable to the Food and Drug Administration for many toxicology endpoints.

In these cases, the most appropriate course of action is neither to assume that nonanimal methods will be easily produced nor to be resigned to the continued use of animals. Rather, it is incumbent on investigators and research-supporting institutions to make the replacement of animals a priority.

3. For many applications, the replacement of animal use occurs most appropriately not through a specific alternative method, but by a substantially different approach to the clinical problem at hand. For example, some research centers are assessing the toxic effects of recreational psychoactive drugs by testing them on animals. Another strategy relies on assessing their effects through noninvasive neurological and psychometric testing on humans who have been using such compounds voluntarily.

The Need for Discussion and Collaboration

To address the ethical and practical issues raised by animal research, scientists and research-sponsoring institutions benefit from information sharing, discussion, and debate representing a wide variety of opinions. Toward that end, governmental bodies in the U.S. (e.g., the Environmental Protection Agency) and abroad dealing with animal testing issues have implemented policies that ensure that animal welfare advocates and scientists advocating for alternatives to animal tests are represented on scientific and regulatory panels.

The process of replacing animals in research, testing, and education is supported by studies showing that routine laboratory procedures and typical laboratory environments are more stressful for animals than is commonly appreciated.

In recent years, it has become clear that viewpoints vary greatly on this issue and are highly mutable as new information comes forward. It is helpful to recognize that, generally speaking, implementing nonanimal methods is neither a simple matter nor a theoretical impossibility. While animal welfare considerations mandate a commitment to the replacement of animals, there are areas for which alternatives have not yet been developed or have not yet gained acceptance by regulatory bodies. The impediments to their development and acceptance relate to both technical difficulties and attitudinal issues. In the course of scientific inquiry, many investigators have credited the use of animals with the elucidation of key points, and it remains a matter of conjecture as to whether the same discoveries could have been accomplished by other means. In contrast, the use of animals in education has undergone dramatic changes in the past decade. Most medical schools have eliminated the use of animals from their curricula, and instructional methods at other educational levels have also evolved in the face of changing technologies. A reasonable viewpoint, we believe, is for investigators and institutions using animals to explore and implement nonanimal methods with all due haste and without limit, recognizing that in some cases the practical challenges inherent in doing so are considerable.

PCRM [Physicians Committee for Responsible Medicine] should continue and expand collaborative efforts to address the need for alternatives to animal use. In cooperation with physicians at Harvard University and the Massachusetts General Hospital, PCRM developed educational materials demonstrating clinical alternatives to animal use in medical instruction, and progress in implementing alternatives has been documented in surveys published by PCRM physicians in the *Journal of Medical Education* and *Academic Medicine*. PCRM toxicologists have served on scientific panels for the Environmental Protection Agency and on the Board of Directors of the Toxicology Excellence for Risk Assessment. PCRM physicians have published invited papers on animal research issues in *Scientific American* and *Lancet Oncology*. Working with outside scientists, PCRM developed a new laboratory technique for assaying insulin that provides alternatives to the ascites method for producing monoclonal antibodies and to the use of fetal calf serum for in-vitro cellular growth. These efforts complement PCRM's primary research work, which focuses on clinical trials in human participants, and are enriched by communication and collaboration with other research organizations.

The Challenges Are Great

The process of replacing animals in research, testing, and education is supported by studies showing that routine laboratory procedures and typical laboratory environments are more stressful for animals than is commonly appreciated. Nonetheless, the challenges of replacing animals are often considerable, raising major scientific, economic, and regulatory issues.

The exploration and implementation of nonanimal methods should be a priority for investigators and research institutions and should take advantage of a wide variety of viewpoints to ensure progress toward scientific, human health, and animal protection goals.

8

It Is Not Possible to Completely Replace Animals in Medical Research

Speaking of Research

Speaking of Research is an advocacy group that seeks to provide accurate information about the importance of animal testing in medical and veterinary science.

It has been suggested that several alternative technologies, including computer modeling, micro-dosing, and MRI scanning, will eventually replace the use of animals in medical research. Strong incentives exist to develop research models that do not require animals. Animal testing is expensive, and researchers are required by law to explore alternatives. However, animal testing does provide significant benefits that are not easily replicated. While alternative technologies will reduce the reliance on animals for testing, they cannot replace animal testing altogether.

Animal rights groups have long propagated the myth that animal research could be replaced tomorrow by a plethora of "alternatives," from computer modeling and micro-dosing to MRI scanning and *in vitro* testing.

So, why the quotation marks on "alternatives"? The fact is that such methods currently tend to complement, rather than replace, the use of animals in research. For instance, computer modeling is a useful tool in the development of a new drug;

however animal research will often be crucial in the creation of the computer program itself. Before looking at some of the reasons that these "alternatives" are not yet sophisticated enough to replace animal research it is important to consider the following two facts:

1. Animal research is very expensive. Animals must be housed, fed and cared for by trained animal welfare technicians and veterinarians. By comparison, replacement methods tend to be much cheaper and thus academic researchers (who compete for limited available funds) and pharmaceutical companies (who are profit-seeking) will prefer to use these cheaper replacements wherever possible. The fact that animal research continues is testament to the fact that for some research there are no alternatives to the use of animals.

2. Replacements to animal research must be used, by law, wherever possible. The Animal Welfare Regulations [2.31] explain the role of Institutional Animal Care and Use Committee (IACUC—every research institute must have one) in ensuring that researchers have considered (and will use) any replacement method available: "The principal investigator [researcher] has considered alternatives to procedures . . . and has provided a written narrative description . . . to determine that alternatives were not available." The fact that animal research continues is once again testament to the fact that there are no alternatives to animal research.

Computer Modeling Can Play an Important Role

"Computers can do amazing things. But even the most powerful computers can't replace animal experiments in medical research."—*Professor Stephen hawking, quoted by Seriously Ill for Medical Research in 1996*

Computer modeling plays an important part in the research process, however its capacity to replace the use of animals is limited. Before one can program a computer model to reflect an aspect of our physiology, an understanding of the physiology being modeled is needed. This knowledge tends to come through research using animals. So animals are needed before we even get to the computer.

Computers are also limited by their processing power. A recent simulation of just half a mouse's brain required the use of the world's fastest supercomputer—Blue Gene/L (300% faster than the second fastest super computer). However the simulation was far from a perfect representation [as BBC News reported on April 27, 2007]:

> The vast complexity of the simulation meant that it was only run for 10 seconds at a speed ten times slower than real life—the equivalent of one second in a real mouse brain.

> The researchers say that although the simulation shared some similarities with a mouse's mental makeup in terms of nerves and connections it lacked the structures seen in real mice brains.

Most scientists do not have access to supercomputers on the scale of Blue Gene/L, which are needed to attempt more complex simulations.

It is an unrealistic hope, and a false claim, that microdosing can replace the use of animals in scientific research wholesale.

Computer simulations of organs have some use, but, unlike *in vivo* research, they are generally forced to focus on major interactions at the cost of minor ones. A simulation of a heart may appear to reproduce the movement of muscles used in pumping blood, but will likely be at the cost of minor reactions and interactions going on within an individual cell.

Professor Dennis Noble, who was part of the team at Oxford University designing a virtual heart, said: "Because hundreds of millions of differential equations are simultaneously being solved, it may take 30 hours just to do a few beats of the heart." But [Noble] denied that his research could completely replace animal research. "I would say the real benefit of the model is that it can do a preliminary filter of your compounds, and that can replace some of the very early stages in animal experimentation". . . .

A drug might work fine on a cell in a test tube, but how will it work in a body?. . . We just don't know whether it would work for sure until we try it on a living creature.

Micro-Dosing Will Not Replace Animal Testing

Micro-dosing is an exciting new technique for measuring how very small doses of potential new medicines move around the body. It should be possible to use micro-dosing in humans to reduce the numbers of animals needed to study the effectiveness of new compounds.

However, micro-dosing has limitations. By its very nature, it cannot predict toxicity or side effects that occur at higher 'therapeutic' doses. It is an unrealistic hope, and a false claim, that micro-dosing can replace the use of animals in scientific research wholesale. This was confirmed recently by the respected organization FRAME (Fund for the Replacement of Animals in Medical Experiments), which stated in this context: *"animal studies will still be required"* [in *ATLA* (Alternatives to Laboratory Animals), 2005].

In Vitro Testing Is Useful in Many Situations

In vitro testing means testing things in a test tube, on the micro level. Dr Phil Stephens has pioneered an *in vitro* test for ulcer treatments based on genetic manipulation. He says: "There are a number of different animal models out there, but they are not really good models for these wounds. So, we began developing an in vitro system."

This is a great example of *replacement*. Scientists always want a better model for their experiments so as to get better (more accurate) results. If a non-animal method can work better than an animal method, great! Not only does it yield better results, it's a lot cheaper, too. However, Dr Stephens also notes: "The in vitro system is not going to replace the animal models, but it will enable a vast number of pre-screens to be undertaken, hopefully vastly reducing the number of animal experiments that go on."

Again, although the aim is to *refine* the models and *reduce* the number of animal experiments, Stephens notes that *in vitro* testing cannot *replace* animal testing altogether. The reasons for this are fairly straightforward: a drug might work fine on a cell in a test tube, but how will it work in a body? A test tube has no blood circulatory system, no liver, no brain, and no nervous system at all. A test tube cannot feel pain or get pregnant. We just don't know whether it would work for sure until we try it on a living creature. And again, it's either animals, or us, that we have to trial the drugs on next.

MRI Scanning Will Reduce, Not Replace, the Need for Animals

Professor Chris Higgins uses MRI imaging to reduce the number of animal experiments needed: "One area we are looking at is what controls appetite and satiety. To do this in the traditional way, we would have to dissect the animal brain, but to avoid this we use in vivo imaging to look at the areas of the brain related to hunger and satiety."

Rapid advances in technology have allowed us to get to the stage where scientists can use scanning to see how certain parts of the brain "light up" under certain conditions, giving us clues about what parts of the brain control different aspects of our bodies, thoughts, cravings, and so on, and clues about how the brain works. However, Prof Higgins goes on: "The one thing that is difficult to do is to understand the genetic and the underlying molecular basis of obesity, and for this we need to use animals, mainly mice, if we are going to develop more effective therapies."

So again, although this 'alternative' can fulfill a useful role and help *reduce* the number of animals used, it cannot replace animal research altogether. Watching how the brain works can help us understand part of the problem, but it also occurs on the genetic and molecular level, which MRI scans cannot show us.

MRI scans may show us a problem in the brain, but animal research is likely needed to fix the problem. We cannot alter a human brain between MRI scans in an attempt to find a cure, so we must use animals first, to ensure the method's safety.

9

The Animal Welfare Act Protects Animals from Abuse in Scientific Research

Richard L. Crawford

Richard L. Crawford is a veterinarian. He works for the Animal Welfare Information Center of the US Department of Agriculture (USDA).

The Animal Welfare Act is administered by the US Department of Agriculture. The act ensures that animals being used for research must be cared for in humane conditions by a licensed veterinarian or other appropriately trained personnel, and in accordance with currently accepted professional practice for a particular circumstance or condition.

The requirements of the Animal Welfare Act are set forth under the Regulations and Standards in the Code of Federal Regulations (CFR). These requirements are found in Title 9 C.F.R., Chapter 1, Subchapter A—Animal Welfare, Parts 1, 2, and 3.... Section numbers are given for reference to the actual wording of each requirement....

I. Title 9 C.F.R., Section 2.33—Attending Veterinarian and Adequate Veterinary Care

(a) Each research facility must have an attending veterinarian who is required to provide adequate veterinary care to the facilities' animals (Sect. 2.33(a)). Adequate Veterinary

Richard L Crawford, "A Quick Reference of the Responsibilities & Functions of the Attending Veterinarians for Research Facilities under the Animal Welfare Act," United States Department of Agriculture, February 29, 2012.

Care is usually determined as what is currently the accepted professional practice or treatment for that particular circumstance or condition.

(1) The attending veterinarian is to be employed under formal arrangements with the research facility. If the attending veterinarian is on a part-time or consulting basis, there must be a written program of veterinary care with a list of regularly scheduled visits to the research facility. The scheduled visits must be appropriate and frequent enough to provide adequate veterinary care to all animals at all times. The schedule should consider the number of animals, the species of animals, the type of housing for the animals, the type of work or research done on the animals, the possibility, or level, of pain or distress that may be involved, and any other conditions or factors that may affect the animals well-being (Sect. 2.33(a)(1)).

(2) The research facility must provide the attending veterinarian with sufficient and appropriate authority to ensure that adequate veterinary care is provided at all times and that he or she is able to oversee the adequacy of all aspects of animal care and use for all animals (Sect. 2.33(a)(2)).

(3) The attending veterinarian must be a voting member of the Institutional Animal Care and Use Committee (IACUC) and have direct or delegated responsibility for the animals at the research facility. If more than one veterinarian is employed by the research facility the attending veterinarian may appoint another veterinarian to the IACUC. The appointed veterinarian must have delegated responsibilities for activities involving animals. A veterinarian engaged principally in research does not meet this requirement (Sect. 2.33(a)(3)).

(b) The research facility must establish and maintain programs of adequate veterinary care that include the following (Sect. 2.33(b)).

(1) That appropriate facilities, personnel, equipment, and services are available so as to comply with requirements (Sect. 2.33(b)(1)).

(2) The use of appropriate methods to control, prevent, diagnose, and treat diseases and injuries. Weekend, holiday, and emergency care must be readily available (Sect. 2.33(b)(2)).

(3) Daily observation of all animals to assess their health and well-being. Daily observation of the animals may be accomplished by someone other than the attending veterinarian, provided that a mechanism of direct and frequent communication is established so that timely and accurate information on problems of animal health, behavior, and well-being is conveyed to the attending veterinarian (Sect. 2.33 (b)(3)).

(4) Guidance is to be provided to the principal investigator, and other personnel, involved in the care and use of animals regarding handling, immobilization, anesthesia, analgesia, tranquilization, and euthanasia (Sect. 2.33 (b)(4)).

(5) Adequate pre- and post procedural care is provided in accordance with current established veterinary medical and nursing procedures (Sect. 2.33(b)(5)).

II. Additional Areas of Responsibility for Attending Veterinarians

(1) Membership on the IACUC (Section 2.31).

(b)(3) Of the members of the Committee:

(i) At least one shall be a Doctor of Veterinary Medicine, with training or experience in laboratory animal science and medicine, who has direct or delegated program responsibility for activities involving animals at the research facility (Sect. 2.31 (b)(3)(i)).

(2) Consultation with the principal investigator to minimize pain and distress. Section 2.31(d) in general and section 2.31 (d)(1)(iv) through (xi) specifically.

(d)(1)(iv) Procedures that may cause more than momentary or slight pain or distress to the animals will:

(A) Be performed with appropriate pain relieving drugs unless withholding such drugs is justified for scientific reasons, in writing, by the principal investigator and will continue only for the necessary period of time.

(B) Involve in their planning, consultation with the attending veterinarian or his or her designee.

(C) Not include the use of paralytics without anesthesia. (This is a flat prohibition).

(v) Animals that would otherwise experience severe or chronic pain or distress that cannot be relieved will be painlessly euthanized at the end of the procedure or, if appropriate, during the procedure.

(vi) The animals' living conditions will be appropriate for their species in accordance with standards set forth in 9 CFR, Part 3, and will contribute to their health and comfort. The housing, feeding, and nonmedical care of the animals will be directed by the attending veterinarian or other scientist trained and experienced in the proper care, handling, and use of the species being maintained or studied.

(vii) Medical care for animals will be available and provided as necessary by a qualified veterinarian.

(viii) Personnel conducting procedures on the species being maintained or studied will be appropriately qualified and trained in those procedures.

(ix) Activities that involve surgery must include appropriate provision for pre-operative and post-operative care of the animals in accordance with established veterinary medical and nursing practices.

- All survival surgery will be performed using aseptic procedures, including surgical gloves, masks, sterilized instruments, and aseptic techniques.

- Major operative procedures on non-rodents will be conducted only in facilities intended for that purpose which shall be operated and maintained under aseptic conditions.

- Non major operative procedures, and all surgery on rodents, do not require a dedicated facility but must be performed using aseptic procedures.

- Operative procedures conducted at field sites need not be performed in dedicated facilities but must be performed using aseptic procedures.

(x) No animal will be used in more than one major operative procedure from which it is allowed to recover unless:

(A) Justified for scientific reasons by the principal investigator, in writing.

(B) Required as routine veterinary procedure or to protect the health or well-being of the animal as determined by the attending veterinarian.

(C) In other special circumstances as determined by the Administrator of APHIS on an individual basis.

(xi) Methods of euthanasia used must be in accordance with the definition of the term set forth in 9 CFR, Part 1, Section 1.1, unless a deviation is justified for scientific reasons, in writing, by the investigator. (Recommendations of the AVMA [American Veterinary Medical Association] panel on euthanasia should be followed).

(3) Training and Personnel Qualifications. Section 2.32.

(a) It is the responsibility of the research facility to ensure that all scientists, research technicians, animal technicians, and other personnel involved in animal care, treatment, and use are qualified to perform their duties. This responsibility shall be fulfilled in part through training and instruction to these personnel.(Sect. 2.32(a)).

(b) Training and instruction shall be made available, and the qualifications of personnel reviewed, with sufficient frequency to fulfill the research facilities responsibility. (Sect. 2.32(b)).

(c) Training and instruction of personnel must include guidance in at least the following areas. (Sect. 2.32(c)).

(1) Humane methods of animal maintenance and experimentation, including (Sect. 2.32 (c)(1)):

(i) The basic needs of each species of animal.

(ii) Proper handling and care for the various species of animals used by the facility.

(iii) Proper pre-procedural and post-procedural care of animals.

(iv) Aseptic surgical methods and procedures.

(2) The concept, availability, and use of research or testing methods that limit the use of animals or minimize animal distress. (Sect. 2.32(c)(2)).

(3) Proper use of pain relieving drugs for any species of animals used by the facility. (Sect. 2.32(c)(3)).

(4) Methods whereby deficiencies in animal care and treatment are reported, including deficiencies reported by facility employees (Sect. 2.32 (c)(4)).

(4) Annual report assurances by the research facility. (Section 2.36).

(b)(1) Assure that professionally acceptable standards governing the care, treatment, and use of animals, including appropriate use of pain relieving drugs, prior to, during, and following actual research, teaching, testing, surgery, or experimentation were followed by the research facility. (Sect. 2.36(b)(1)).

(5) Indoor housing facilities for dogs and cats. (Section 3.2).

(a) Heating, cooling, and temperature. . . . When dogs or cats are present, the ambient temperature in the facility must not fall below 50 degrees F for dogs and cats not acclimated to lower temperatures, for those breeds that cannot tolerate lower temperatures without stress or discomfort, and for sick, aged, young, or infirm dogs or cats, except as approved by the attending veterinarian. (Sect. 3.2(a)).

(b) Ventilation. . . . The relative humidity must be maintained at a level that ensures the health and well-being of the dogs and cats housed therein, in accordance with the directions of the attending veterinarian and generally accepted professional and husbandry practices. (Sect. 3.2(b)).

(6) Sheltered housing facilities for dogs and cats. (Section 3.3).

(a) Heating, cooling, and temperature. . . . The ambient temperature in the sheltered part of the facility must not fall below 50 degrees F for dogs and cats not acclimated to lower temperatures, for those breeds that cannot tolerate lower temperatures without stress and discomfort, and for sick, aged, young, or infirm dogs and cats, except as approved by the attending veterinarian. (Sect. 3.3(a)).

(7) Outdoor housing facilities for dogs and cats. (Section 3.4).

(a)(1) The following categories of dogs or cats must not be kept in outdoor facilities unless that practice is specifically approved by the attending veterinarian. (Sect 3.4(a)(1)).

(i) Dogs or cats not acclimated to the temperatures prevalent in the area or region where they are maintained.

(ii) Breeds of dogs or cats that cannot tolerate the prevalent temperatures of the area without stress or discomfort.

(iii) Sick, infirm, aged, or young dogs or cats.

(8) Primary enclosures:(Section 3.6).

(b) Additional requirements for cats.

(1) Space.

(iii) Each queen with nursing kittens must be provided with an additional amount of floor space, based on her breed and behavioral characteristics, and in accordance with generally accepted husbandry practices. If the additional amount of floor space for each nursing kitten is equivalent to less than five percent of the minimum requirement for the queen, such housing must be approved by the attending veterinarian of the research facility (Sect. 3.6 (b)(1)(iii)).

(c) Additional requirements for dogs.

(1) Space.

(ii) Each bitch with nursing puppies must be provided with an additional amount of floor space, based on her breed and behavioral characteristics, and in accordance with generally accepted husbandry practices as determined by the attending veterinarian. If the additional amount of floor space for each nursing puppy is less than five percent of the minimum requirement for the bitch, such housing must be approved by the attending veterinarian of the research facility (Sect. 3.6 (c)(1)(ii)).

(9) Compatible grouping. (Section 3.7).

(e) Dogs or cats that have or are suspected of having a contagious disease must be isolated from healthy animals in the colony, as directed by the attending veterinarian (Sect. 3.7 (e)).

(10) Exercise for dogs. (Section 3.8).

Research facilities must develop, document, and follow an appropriate plan to provide dogs with the opportunity for exercise. The plan must be approved by the attending veterinarian and must include written standard procedures to be followed in providing the opportunity for exercise.

(b) Dogs housed in groups (Sect. 3.8 (b))....Such animals may be maintained in compatible groups unless:

(2) In the opinion of the attending veterinarian, such housing would adversely affect the health or well-being of the dogs (Sect. 3.8 (b)(2)).

(c) Methods and period of providing exercise opportunity (Sect. 3.8(c)).

(1) The frequency, method, and duration of the opportunity for exercise shall be determined by the attending veterinarian and, at research facilities, in consultation with and approval by the Committee (Sect. 3.8(c)(1)).

(d) Exemptions (Sect. 3.8 (d)).

(1) If, in the opinion of the attending veterinarian, it is inappropriate for certain dogs to exercise because of their health, condition, or well-being, the dealer, exhibitor, or research facility may be exempted from meeting the requirements for exercise for those dogs. Such exemption must be documented by the attending veterinarian and, unless the basis for exemption is a permanent condition, must be reviewed at least every 30 days.

(11) Feeding of dogs and cats (Section 3.9).

(a) Dogs and cats must be fed at least once each day, except as otherwise might be required to provide adequate veterinary care. . . .

(12) Watering of dogs and cats (Section 3.10).

If potable water is not continually available to the dogs and cats, it must be offered to the dogs and cats as often as necessary to ensure their health and well-being, but not less than twice daily for at least one hour each time, unless restricted by the attending veterinarian. . . . (See also sections 3.30 and 3.55).

(13) Indoor housing facilities for nonhuman primates (Section 3.76).

(a) Heating, cooling, and temperature. . . . The ambient temperature must be maintained at a level that ensures the health and well-being of the species housed, as directed by the attending veterinarian, in accordance with generally accepted professional and husbandry practices (Sect. 3.76 (a)).

(b) Ventilation. . . . The relative humidity maintained must be at a level that ensures the health and well-being of the animals housed, as directed by the attending veterinarian, in accordance with generally accepted professional and husbandry practices (Sect. 3.76 (b)).

(14) Sheltered housing facilities for nonhuman primates (Section 3.77).

(a) Heating, cooling, and temperature. . . . The ambient temperature in the sheltered, part of the facility must not fall below 45 degrees F for more than four consecutive hours when nonhuman primates are present, and must not rise above 85 degrees F for more than four consecutive hours when nonhuman primates are present, unless temperatures above 85 degrees F are approved by the attending veterinarian, in accordance with generally accepted husbandry practices. The ambient temperature must be maintained at a level that ensures the health and well-being of the species housed, as directed by the attending veterinarian, in accordance with generally accepted professional and husbandry practices (Sect. 3.77(a)).

(b) Ventilation. . . . The relative humidity maintained must be at a level that ensures the health and well-being of the species housed, as directed by the attending veterinarian, in accordance with generally accepted professional and husbandry practices (Sect. 3.77(b)).

(15) Outdoor housing facilities for nonhuman primates (Section 3.78).

(a) Acclimation. Only nonhuman primates that are acclimated, as determined by the attending veterinarian, to the prevailing temperature and humidity at the outdoor housing facility during the time of year they are at the facility, and can tolerate the range of temperatures and climatic conditions known to occur at the facility at that time of year without stress or discomfort, may be kept in outdoor facilities (Sect. 3.78(a)).

(b) Shelter from the elements. . . . The shelter must safely provide heat to the nonhuman primates to prevent the ambient temperature from falling below 45 degrees F, except as directed by the attending veterinarian, and in accordance with generally accepted professional and husbandry practices (Sect. 3.78(b)).

(16) Mobile or traveling housing facilities for nonhuman primates (Section 3.79).

(a) Heating, cooling, and temperature. . . . The ambient temperature must be maintained at a level that ensures the health and well-being of the species housed, as directed by the attending veterinarian, in accordance with generally accepted professional and husbandry practices (Sect. 3.79 (a)).

(17) Primary enclosures for nonhuman primates (Section 3.80).

(b) Minimum space requirements.

(2) On and after February 15, 1994.

(iii) In the case of research facilities any exemption from these standards must be required by a research proposal or in the judgment of the attending veterinarian and must be approved by the Committee (Sect. 3.80 (b)(2)(iii)).

(18) Environmental enhancement and psychological well-being of nonhuman primates (Section 3.81).

Research facilities must develop, document, and follow an appropriate plan for environmental enhancement adequate to promote the psychological well-being of nonhuman primates. The plan must be in accordance with the currently accepted professional standards as cited in appropriate professional journals or reference guides, as directed by the attending veterinarian. . . .

(a) Social grouping. The environmental enhancement plan must include specific provisions to address the social needs of nonhuman primates of species known to exist in social groups in nature. Such provisions must be in accordance with currently accepted professional standards, as cited in appropriate professional journals or reference guides, and as directed by the attending veterinarian. The plan may provide for the following exceptions (Sect. 3.81(a)).

(2) Nonhuman primates that have or are suspected of having a contagious disease must be isolated from healthy animals in the colony as directed by the attending veterinarian (Sect. 3.81 (a)(2)).

(3) Compatibility of nonhuman primates must be determined in accordance with generally accepted professional practices and actual observations, as directed by the attending veterinarian, to ensure that the nonhuman primates are in fact compatible. Individually housed nonhuman primates must be able to see and hear nonhuman primates of their own or compatible species unless the attending veterinarian determines that it would endanger their health, safety, or well-being (Sect. 3.81 (a)(3)).

(c) Special considerations. Certain nonhuman primates must be provided special attention regarding enhancement of their environment, based on the needs of the individual species and in accordance with the instructions of the attending veterinarian. Nonhuman primates requiring special attention are the following (Sect. 3.81 (c)):

(1) Infants and young juveniles.

(2) Those that show signs, of being in psychological distress through behavior or appearance.

(3) Those used in research for which the Committee-approved protocol requires restricted activity.

(4) Individually housed nonhuman primates that are unable to see and hear nonhuman primates of their own or compatible species.

(5) Great apes weighing over 110 lbs. Research facilities must include in the environmental enhancement plan special provisions for great apes weighing over 110 lbs., including additional opportunities to express species typical behavior.

(d) Restraint devices. Nonhuman primates must not be maintained in restraint devices unless required for health reasons as determined by the attending veterinarian or by a research proposal approved by the Committee at the research facility (Sect. 3.81(d)).

(e) Exemptions.

(1) The attending veterinarian may exempt an individual nonhuman primate from participation in the environmental enhancement plan because of its health or condition, or in consideration of its well-being. The basis of the exemption must be recorded by the

attending veterinarian for each exempted nonhuman primate. Unless the basis for the exemption is a permanent condition, the exemption must be reviewed every 30 days by the attending veterinarian (Sect. 3.81 (e)(1)).

(19) Feeding nonhuman primates (Section 3.82 (b)).

Nonhuman primates must be fed at least once each day except as otherwise might be required to provide adequate veterinary care.

(20) Watering for nonhuman primates (Section 3.83).

Potable water must be provided in sufficient quantity to every nonhuman primate housed at the facility. If potable water is not continually available to the nonhuman primates, it must be offered to them as often as necessary to ensure their health and well-being, but not less than twice daily for at least one hour each time, unless otherwise required by the attending veterinarian, or as required by the research proposal approved by the Committee at the research facility.

(21) Consignment to Carriers and Intermediate Handlers (Section 3.86).

(c) .... Food and water instructions must be provided and attached to the outside of the primary enclosure so that it is easily noticed. Instructions for no food or water are not acceptable unless directed by the attending veterinarian. . .

10

The Animal Welfare Act Does Not Protect Animals from Abuse in Research

Stop Animal Exploitation NOW!

Stop Animal Exploitation NOW! (SAEN) was founded in 1996 to force an end to the abuse of animals in laboratories.

Although the Animal Welfare ACT (AWA) contains provisions that are intended to protect animals from abuse, the US Department of Agriculture regularly documents serious violations of the act by research institutions. In addition, research institutions also have the option of exempting some animals from the protections of the AWA, if they can document that such exemptions were necessary for scientific reasons. Documentation shows that such exemptions are extremely common, and decisions about the exemptions are made by those employed by the research institutions.

The use of all animals, including non-human primates, is regulated by the Animal Welfare Act (AWA). This law, enacted in the 1960s, now includes requirements for housing, diet, veterinary care, psychological enrichment, and experimental procedures. This law is enforced by the United States Department of Agriculture (USDA) through the Animal Care division of the Animal & Plant Health Inspection Service (APHIS).

Stop Animal Exploitation NOW! "The Abuse of Non-Human Primates in Federally Regulated Laboratories: October 2011: Are Non-Human Primates Protected from Abuse in U.S. Laboratories?" October 2011. Copyright © 2011 by Stop Animal Exploitation Now! All rights reserved. Reproduced by permission.

However, questions exist regarding the effectiveness of this law. Is this law even followed? Have U.S. laboratories seriously violated this law involving primates? Do the regulations which arise from this law actually protect non-human primates from abusive practices? Some recent examples of violations are listed below. This is followed by a section that discusses legally allowable "exceptions."

One section of the Animal Welfare Act that is specific to non-human primates is section 3.81 Environmental Enhancement to Promote Psychological Well-Being. A search of the USDA Animal Care database reveals that in the last 12 months 16 facilities violated the Environmental Enhancement requirements of the Animal Welfare Act.

USDA Inspection Reports of Serious Primate Abuse Within Registered Research Facilities

A USDA inspection report dated 8/2/11 cites McLean Hospital (Boston, MA) for an incident in which a primate was found dead after only 10 minutes in an experimental chamber. The lab is cited for insufficient supervision of experimentation, as well as inadequate housing and insufficient environmental enhancement for primates.

> [Citations against Princeton University] include inadequate functioning by the Institutional Animal Care & Use Committee (a repeat violation), inadequate watering, and the filing of a fraudulent report with the USDA.

A July 19, 2011, USDA inspection report cites the Harvard Medical School five times for violations including unqualified personnel, inadequate supervision of experimentation by the lab's Institutional Animal Care & Use Committee, and inadequate housing for primates. Several of the citations were directly relevant to a February 2011 incident in which a nonhuman primate was given an overdose of anesthetic causing irreversible renal failure requiring euthanasia. This is just over a year after a June 9, 2010 incident at a Harvard Medical School facility in which a dead non-human primate was found in an enclosure which had just gone through a cage-washing machine.

A USDA inspection report from May of 2010 reveals an incident during which eight marmosets escaped from a cage at the University of Massachusetts, Amherst (UMASS). While running loose, they pulled an infant marmoset through the bars of a cage which housed another group. The infant died as a result of this incident. UMASS was cited for inadequate primary enclosures. UMASS was cited for several other AWA violations including inadequate supervision of experiments by the lab's Institutional Animal Care & Use Committee as well as inadequate housing/facilities.

An August 3, 2011, USDA report reveals that improper animal handling at MPI Research (Mattawan, MI) caused severe traumatic injuries to four animals. The injuries to these animals were so severe that no treatment was possible, requiring euthanasia. USDA sources have confirmed that two of these animals were non-human primates.

In an April 27, 2011 USDA inspection report Princeton University is repeatedly cited for experiments that deprive monkeys of access to water. The citations include inadequate functioning by the Institutional Animal Care & Use Committee (a repeat violation), inadequate watering, and the filing of a fraudulent report with the USDA. In an unrelated incident the lab is also cited for inadequately observing a marmoset who was giving birth. Princeton was the target of a scathing USDA inspection report of June 23, 2010. In issuing 13 separate citations against Princeton, the USDA focused on the same highly invasive project which deprives primates of water and implants devices into the skull.

Princeton University has also been the target of a recent whistleblower who disclosed major Animal Welfare Act violations including primate deaths through malnutrition, deaths due to lack of veterinary care, and other primates being killed in a cagewasher. . . .

A May, 2011, USDA inspection report for the University of Rochester, School of Medicine, and Dentistry reveals citations for depriving several primates of food for extended periods. Primate #940 was starved for 4 days and primate #631 was denied food for two days. The University is also cited for filing fraudulent reports for not listing these animals as experiencing distress. In a news story university staff admitted that the food deprivation was done intentionally and was not part of an experimental protocol.

A June, 2011, USDA inspection report cites Vanderbilt repeatedly for the performance of illegal, unapproved and highly invasive brain surgeries on at least one primate by unapproved and unqualified surgeon(s). The USDA report cites Vanderbilt repeatedly for incidents surrounding experimentation on primate #4414. An unapproved, and botched, surgical procedure was attempted by an unapproved surgeon in September of 2010. Further illegal surgeries and other illegal procedures were performed on the same primate in December of 2010 and April of 2011.

A USDA report dated 5/31/11 cited the University of Louisiana, Lafayette, for: ". . . deaths of 3 Rhesus monkeys which became trapped in a chute in one of the outdoor breeding colonies. The remains were autolyzed therefore they had been trapped for some time and not properly monitored."

Examples of USDA Official Warnings and Fines

In June of 2011 the Lovelace Respiratory Research Institute of Albuquerque (NM) was fined $21,750 by the USDA for several violations including inadequate housing because an infant cynomolgous monkey had escaped, and another primate became trapped and suffocated.

In March of 2011 the University of Washington, Seattle, paid a $10,893 fine for violations which involved the deaths of three non-human primates, one from malnutrition, and two from infection of cranial implants.

An Official Warning made public by the USDA in July of 2011 revealed that the Weill Medical College of Cornell University killed a non-human primate through lung hyperinflation when a breathing tube was kept clamped during a surgical procedure.

Animals such as primates can be exempted from requirements for feeding, watering, cage cleaning, social housing, etc.

In September of 2010 Northwestern University received an Official Warning from the USDA for a thermal injury (burn) to a non-human primate during a tail amputation procedure.

In July of 2010 Vanderbilt University was fined $8156 for multiple violations of the AWA, including an incident in which an infant galago monkey was found dead in bedding that had been run through a washing machine.

A January, 2011, Official Warning cited the Southern Research Institute for the death of a primate whose head had become caught in a cage. . . .

The Animal Welfare Act Allows for Numerous Exemptions

Basic standards for care and treatment are a major part of the Animal Welfare Act (AWA). These standards include frequency of feeding, watering, cage cleaning, social housing, frequency of surgical procedures, etc. However, the AWA also allows animals to be exempted from these standards for 'scientific' reasons. And so, animals such as primates can be exempted from requirements for feeding, watering, cage cleaning, social housing, etc. Essentially they can be placed outside the coverage of the law in these areas. Is this done very often? Does it involve a substantial number of animals?

The committees empowered to approve protocols which exempt animals from Animal Welfare Act regulations are comprised of employees of the institutions that receive funding to perform the experiments.

While it would be difficult to answer this question fully, due to the number of laboratories that utilize primates, it is possible to get a snapshot of this situation by examining a relatively small number of the larger primate facilities. The facilities examined are: Emory University, Harvard Medical School, University of Louisiana (Lafayette), the National Institutes of Health, Oregon Health Sciences University, the University of Wisconsin (Madison), and Wake Forest University. Individually, these labs run the spectrum on these issues, but one example should suffice. Emory University exempted 1835 primates from the standards of the AWA. 4 primates were used in painful experiments without anesthesia. 381 primates experienced restraint (i.e. confinement in a primate restraint chair). 1356 primates, were singly housed, exempting them from having social contact with members of their own species. 94 primates had restricted access to either food or water. Emory used a total of 2369 primates in experimentation. This means that 77% of the primates used in experimentation at Emory were exempted from the standards of the Animal Welfare Act.

Collectively, these labs experimented on 15,324 primates or 21.5% of the national total, or slightly over 1 out of every 5. These labs exempted 6273 animals (as listed in the exceptions to standard care section of their annual reports) to at least one of the standards contained in the AWA. This could mean that these animals were prevented from having access to food/water for extended periods, or they may have been exempted from socialization, or housing standards, cage cleaning standards, etc. This accounts for 41% of the primates used at these facilities. If this statistic is generalized to the national total then 29,240 primates were exempted from at least one regulation that is part of the Animal Welfare Act. Additionally, USDA national statistics for 2010 indicate that 1395 non-human primates or 2% were used in painful/stressful experiments without benefit of anesthesia. In total, then, an estimated 43% of all non-human primates used in experimentation are legally excluded from at least some level of protection under the Animal Welfare Act.

Who decides on these exceptions? These practices are approved by the Institutional Animal Care and Use Committees which are mandated by the AWA and charged with the responsibility of approving all animal experimentation within a facility. These committees are routinely comprised almost entirely of staff that is employed at the facility at which the experimentation will be conducted. These committees are required to have only one member who represents the views of the community. In other words, the committees empowered to approve protocols which exempt animals from Animal Welfare Act regulations are comprised of employees of the institutions that receive funding to perform the experiments. These individuals have a vested interest in approving experiments because that keeps the federal funding rolling into their employer.

11

Animal Welfare Is Different Than Animal Rights

Texas Society for Biomedical Research

The Texas Society for Biomedical Research (TSBR) was founded in 1989 in response to intensifying animal rights activism. It is a private nonprofit organization whose mission is to promote research and education in the biomedical sciences. Members come from academia, industry, nonprofit research, education and advocacy organizations, professional societies, and philanthropic foundations.

In the United States, laws have been enacted to ensure that animals in research laboratories and professional kennels are treated humanely. Animal welfare refers to standards of animal care that were created through laws. Animal rights is distinct from animal welfare. The philosophy of animal rights places humans and animals on the same moral level and holds that it is wrong to cause suffering in animals in order to obtain a human good. Animal rights activists oppose animal experimentation of all kinds, the use of animals for food or to make clothing, and the use of animals as pets.

Animal welfare endorses the responsible use of animals to satisfy certain human needs—from companionship and sport, to uses that involve the taking of life, such as for food, clothing, and medical research. Animal welfare advocates seek to ensure that all animals used by humans have their basic needs fulfilled in terms of food, shelter, and health, and that they experience no unnecessary suffering in providing for human needs.

Texas Society for Biomedical Research, "Animal Welfare and Animal Rights," 2011. http://www.tsbr.org/content/animal-welfare-and-animal-rights.

Animal welfare is a term that came into use after the federal Animal Welfare Act passed in 1966. The term is used by research compliance inspectors employed by the government, by those who work in shelters, and by veterinarians and scientists employed by companies, hospitals, and universities that perform animal research, all of whom are charged with ensuring that detailed regulations are followed when using animals in research. People who promote animal welfare believe in the controlled use of animals in research under the strict guidelines of the Animal Welfare Act and its numerous amendments. Proactive animal welfare advocates also adopt the same high standards for the use of rats, mice, and birds in research, which are not presently included in the Animal Welfare Act as currently amended.

The American Veterinary Medical Association Policy on Animal Welfare and Animal Rights describes animal welfare as ". . . a human responsibility that encompasses all aspects of animal well-being, including proper housing, management, nutrition, disease prevention and treatment, responsible care, humane handling, and, when necessary, humane euthanasia."

In the animal welfare view . . . humankind's right to use animals for human benefit carries with it the responsibility to do so humanely.

Although many cultures have vastly differing views and traditions of animal use, most western societies have adopted basic rules governing human behavior toward animals. In the U.S., laws have been enacted at the federal level to assure the welfare of animals in medical research labs as well as the health of dogs and cats raised in professional kennels. These laws are administered by the U.S. Department of Agriculture.

In addition, most communities have local laws and ordinances to protect animals from unnecessary cruelty. These rules address everything from pet neglect and abuse to the treatment of circus animals, and from hunting and fishing to meatpacking. Without addressing the issue of whether animals have inherent rights, our society has enacted laws to govern the behavior of human beings in their interaction with animals.

In the animal welfare view, social traditions and the body of existing law with respect to our use of animals are based on the premise that humankind's right to use animals for human benefit carries with it the responsibility to do so humanely. These traditions and laws exist because for centuries man has recognized the wisdom and natural correctness of using animals for food, clothing, research, education, and companionship.

The first animal welfare organization, the Royal Society for the Prevention of Cruelty to Animals (RSPCA), was founded in 1824 in London to promote the protection of domestic animals.

The RSPCA's American counterpart, the American Society for the Prevention of Cruelty to Animals (ASPCA), was founded in New York City in 1866 by Henry Bergh, who was concerned about cruelty to horses, stray cats, and dogs. The ASPCA notes that in 1952, it initiated "voluntary inspection of laboratories in New York that use animals for research," an important function that is performed today by the Association for Assessment and Accreditation of Laboratory Animal Care (AAALAC).

Animal Rights Advocates Attempt to Protect Animals from All Suffering

Animal rights, as a philosophical viewpoint, is fundamentally different from animal welfare, since it maintains that animals are not ours to use at all—for food, clothing, entertainment, or experimentation.

Some people use the term "animal rights" as a shorthand for "better conditions for animals", but animal rights actually means much more. At the center of the animal rights philosophy is the belief that animals must be included within the same system of morals that are applied to people.

Many adherents further argue for equality—that animal rights should parallel basic human rights, including the right to life and to freedom from ownership and confinement, and from use as a food source or subject of experimentation without consent.

In the animal rights view . . . the question is whether humans have the right to exploit other sentient beings for any purpose.

The key point is "sentience," or the capacity to experience pain or pleasure. In the animal rights view, if a being is capable of suffering, there can be no moral justification for refusing to take that suffering into consideration. No matter the nature of the being, the principle of equality requires that its suffering be counted equally with the like suffering of any other being.

In the animal rights view, the question is not merely whether an animal suffers as a consequence of any particular animal use. The question is whether humans have the right to exploit other sentient beings for any purpose. Even if a particular type of animal use is considered "humane" by traditional definitions, the fact that the animal has the capacity to suffer is sufficient to make its use unacceptable.

Therefore, a believer in animal rights would directly compare the needs of animals against the needs of people instead of putting the needs of animals second. He or she might decide that it is wrong to perform a medical procedure that sacrificed an animal, even if it saved a human life, because that would violate the animal's right to life. As with animal welfare, individuals' beliefs about animal rights vary.

"Animal Rights" as a movement has its origin in the 1970s, following the publication of Peter Singer's book, *Animal Lib-*

eration, in 1975 that drew comparisons between discrimination against humans (racism) and discrimination against animals (speciesism).

The basic "platform" of animal rights calls for the end to all human "exploitation" of animals—this includes, but is not limited to:

- Use of animals and animal products for human or animal dietary consumption (meat and dairy)

- Confinement livestock and poultry production

- Hunting, trapping, and fishing

- Fur-farming

- Use of animals in cosmetic and product-safety testing

- The practice of owning pets

- Use of animals and animal products in clothing and domestic products (wool, fur, leather, silk)

- Use of animals for any medical or veterinary research or procedure

- Zoos, circuses, rodeos, horseshows, and dog-shows

- All performing animals

- Guide-dogs for the blind

- Police dogs and search and rescue dogs

There are thousands of animal rights groups in the U.S. They vary greatly in the type of opposition to the varying uses of animals and in how they oppose these uses. Some groups only oppose using animals in research; some oppose the use of animal products in clothing (leather shoes, fur coats, wool sweaters, silk shirts, etc). Some animal rights advocates believe that animal welfare reforms impede progress toward animal rights because they improve the conditions under which "animal exploitation" occurs, making it more difficult to stimulate public opposition. Methods of protest vary from educational outreach in elementary schools, to media campaigns, to vandalism, arson, harassment, and physical attacks.

In the spring of 2002, the FBI declared two activist groups, the Animal Liberation Front and the Earth Liberation Front, as the top two domestic terrorist groups in the U.S.

12

Americans Need Better Information About Animal Testing of Cosmetics

Abby Ellin

Abby Ellin is a writer whose work has appeared in The New York Times, Newsweek, Salon, *and* The Daily Beast.

The European Union has banned animal testing of cosmetics and personal care products, but it is still legal in the United States. Consumers who want to purchase products that have not been tested on animals may find that product information is confusing and often misleading.

The actress Kristin Bauer, of "True Blood" fame, has an annual ritual when she visits her family home in Racine, Wis.: She takes a black marker and scribbles on the sides of specific products and cosmetics, "Tested on animals."

"It's so simple for me: we shouldn't be torturing another living being for mascara when we don't have to," said Ms. Bauer, a vegetarian who lives in Los Angeles with her husband, Abri van Straten, two dogs and two cats. "It seems so odd when you think of shaving cream and a bunny, or mascara and a guinea pig. We're not saving a life."

More and More Cosmetics Companies Avoid Animal Testing

As a spokeswoman for the Physicians Committee for Responsible Medicine, a nonprofit health organization whose goals

Companies may say their products are "cruelty-free" or "not tested on animals," she said, but their claims might refer only to the finished product, and not to specific ingredients (the bulk of animal testing happens on the ingredient level). Or they hire outside laboratories to do the testing for them.

Even "all-natural" claims are confusing. Michelle Larner, a makeup artist in New York, thought she was using only products not tested on animals because she favors lines aimed at customers with sensitive skin. But then she went to the Web site of the advocacy organization People for the Ethical Treatment of Animals, which lists companies that do and don't test on animals.

"I saw a few brands that fall into the 'natural' range that I just assumed would be cruelty-free," she said. She was dismayed to discover that "everything I use, from mascara, toothpaste, deodorant and feminine products were on the list. Even my laundry cleaning products are on this 'yes' list."

Pressuring Manufacturers to Go "Cruelty-Free"

A majority of items made without animal testing are independent brands that are not readily available at chain drugstores, department stores or specialty stores, she added. It also would be easier "if the products had a disclaimer saying, 'Yes, we test on animals,'" Ms. Larner said. "I would not buy it."

Some organizations have been trying to change that. PETA licenses its "cruelty-free bunny" logo.

Leaping Bunny, a program run by the Coalition for Consumer Information on Cosmetics, licenses a rabbit logo to companies the organization has certified as cruelty-free. It also provides consumers with a list of these companies.

So far, about a third of the 400 certified companies use the logo, said Ms. Katrinak, including Burt's Bees, Tom's of Maine, the Body Shop and Urban Decay. Not everyone, though, thinks that eliminating animal research entirely is feasible. "Most ingredients in cosmetic products were tested long ago, so very little testing is done nowadays," said Frankie Trull, president of the Foundation for Biomedical Research, which promotes humane and responsible animal research. But "in some cases, animal models are still a necessary part of ensuring ingredients will not cause harm to people."

Ms. Bauer, who favors Almay and bareFaced Mineral Cosmetics, is unmoved by this argument. She often checks PETA's Web site to see which products do and don't test on animals.

"It takes five minutes to go through this list," she said. "Sometimes the non-tested are more organic and natural. Sometimes they're even cheaper."

Organizations to Contact

The editors have compiled the following list of organizations concerned with the issues debated in this book. The descriptions are derived from materials provided by the organizations. All have publications or information available for interested readers. The list was compiled on the date of publication of the present volume; names, addresses, phone and fax numbers, and e-mail and Internet addresses may change. Be aware that many organizations take several weeks or longer to respond to inquiries, so allow as much time as possible.

American Anti-Vivisection Society (AAVS)
801 Old York Rd., Suite 204, Jenkintown, PA   19046-1611
(215) 887-0816
e-mail: aavs@aavs.org
website: www.aavs.org

The American Anti-Vivisection Society (AAVS) is a nonprofit animal advocacy and educational organization dedicated to ending experimentation on animals in research, testing, and education. Its website includes extensive information about current practices as well as alternatives to the use of animals in research and education.

American College of Laboratory Animal Medicine (ACLAM)
96 Chester St., Chester, NH   03036
(603) 887-2467 • fax: (603) 887-0096
website: www.aclam.org

The American College of Laboratory Animal Medicine (ACLAM) advances the humane care and responsible use of laboratory animals through certification of veterinary specialists, professional development, education, and research. Its website includes information about career pathways and mentoring, as well as position statements on topics such as adequate veterinary care, animal experimentation, rodent surgery, and pain and distress.

Americans for Medical Progress (AMP)

526 King St., Suite 201, Alexandria, VA   22314
(703) 836-9595
e-mail: amp@amprogress.org
website: www.amprogress.org

Americans for Medical Progress (AMP) provides information to foster a balanced public debate on the animal research issue. Through various specialty publications, outreach initiatives, and the media, AMP seeks to promote understanding of and support for the use of animals in medicine. AMP also distributes news, information, and analysis about animal rights extremism to the research community through its news service.

Animal Liberation Front (ALF)

North American Press Office, 3371 Glendale Blvd. #107
Los Angeles, CA   90039
(213) 640-5048
website: www.animalliberationfront.com

The Animal Liberation Front (ALF) takes direct action against animal abuse by rescuing animals and causing financial loss to animal exploiters, usually through the damage and destruction of property. The ALF Press Office is a source of information about the philosophy and the activities of the organization. The website includes essays, press releases, communiqués, and access to recent news coverage of the organization's activities.

Animal Welfare Institute (AWI)

900 Pennsylvania Ave. SE, Washington, DC   20003
(202) 337-2332 • fax: (202) 446-2131
e-mail: awi@awionline.org
website: www.awionline.org

The Animal Welfare Institute (AWI) seeks to alleviate the suffering inflicted on animals by people. Issues addressed have included animal research and testing, nonanimal alternatives, factory farming, and the fur trade. Information about AWI activities and lists of its publications can be found on the organization's website.

Association for the Assessment and Accreditation of Laboratory Animal Care International (AAALAC)
5283 Corporate Dr., Suite 203, Frederick, MD   21703
(301) 696-9626 • fax: (301) 696-9627
e-mail: accredit@aaalac.org
website: www.aaalac.org

AAALAC International is a private, nonprofit organization that promotes the humane treatment of animals in science through voluntary accreditation and assessment programs. AAALAC's accreditation process enables research programs to demonstrate that they meet the minimum standards required by law and are achieving excellence in animal care and use. The AAALAC website includes a directory of accredited organizations.

Foundation for Biomedical Research (FBR)
818 Connecticut Ave. NW, Suite 303, Washington, DC   20006
(202) 457-0654
website: www.fbresearch.org

The Foundation for Biomedical Research (FBR) works to promote public understanding and support for humane and responsible animal research. Its activities target the news media, teachers, students and parents, pet owners, and other groups to provide accessible, reliable information about animal research.

The Humane Society of the United States
2100 L St. NW, Washington, DC   20037
(202) 452-1100
website: www.humanesociety.org

The Humane Society of the United States rescues and cares for animals and conducts advocacy and education to reduce animal suffering and create meaningful social change for animals. It monitors enforcement of existing laws and educates the public about animal issues. The organization's website includes resources for the animal care community, parents, educators, and students. Publications on the organization's website include *All Animals, Animal Sheltering,* and *Kind News,* a children's magazine.

The Jane Goodall Institute

4245 North Fair, Suite 600, Arlington, VA   22203
(703) 682-9220 • fax: (703) 682-9312
website: www.janegoodall.org

The Jane Goodall Institute is an international organization that empowers people to make a difference for all living things. The institute is especially concerned with improving global understanding and treatment of great apes through research, public education, and advocacy, and with contributing to the preservation of great apes and their habitats by combining conservation with education and the promotion of sustainable livelihoods.

The Johns Hopkins Center for Alternatives to Animal Testing (CAAT)

Bloomberg School of Public Health
Department of Environmental Health Sciences
615 N. Wolfe St., W7032, Baltimore, MD   21205
(410) 614-4990 • fax: (410) 614-2871
e-mail: caat@jhsph.edu
website: http://caat.jhsph.edu

The Johns Hopkins Center for Alternatives to Animal Testing (CAAT) promotes humane science by supporting the creation, development, validation, and use of alternatives to animals in research, product safety testing, and education. CAAT conducts workshops for researchers and corporations. Its website includes a media center, articles on alternatives to animal testing, and information about programs offered by CAAT.

National Institutes of Health (NIH)
9000 Rockville Pike, Bethesda, MD   20892-7982
(301) 496-4000
e-mail: NIHinfo@od.nih.gov
website: www.nih.gov

The National Institutes of Health (NIH), a part of the US Department of Health and Human Services, is the medical research agency of the United States government. It sets policy, makes grants, and monitors ongoing research involving both humans and animals. NIH's website contains a section devoted to animals in research, including resources for the general public. Topics covered include basics of medical research with animals, alternatives to research with animals, stories of animals in action, animal welfare, and information for students and educators.

People for the Ethical Treatment of Animals (PETA)
501 Front St., Norfolk, VA   23510
(757) 622-7382 • fax: (757) 622-0457
website: www.peta.org

PETA is an international animal rights organization that works to establish and protect the rights of all animals. PETA promotes public education, cruelty investigations, animal rescue, and legislative action. It produces fact sheets, brochures, flyers, and a weekly e-newsletter. Many of these publications are available on its website.

Physicians Committee for Responsible Medicine (PCRM)
5100 Wisconsin Ave. NW, Suite 400, Washington, DC   20016
(202) 686-2210
e-mail: pcrm@pcrm.org
website: http://pcrm.org

Physicians Committee for Responsible Medicine (PCRM) is a nonprofit organization that conducts advocacy in support of higher ethical standards in medical research. It promotes alternatives to animal research and animal testing and has worked to end experiments involving animals. The organization also promotes nonanimal methods for medical education. In addition to news releases, fact sheets, and action alerts, PCRM's website covers current topics such as alternatives to using animals in research and testing as well as in education and training; animal's psychological and social lives; and humane charities.

Stop Animal Exploitation NOW! (S.A.E.N.)
PMB 280- 1081-B State Route 28, Milford, OH   45150
(513) 575-5517
e-mail: saen@saenonline.org
website: www.all-creatures.org/saen/index.html

Stop Animal Exploitation NOW! organizes activities aimed at forcing an end to abuse of animals in research laboratories in the United States. The S.A.E.N. website archives recent news articles and reports and posts information about events and campaigns to support an end to the use of animals in biomedical research and testing. The organization also publishes a newsletter, *The Defender*, which is issued on an intermittent basis.

Bibliography

Books

Lynda I.A. Birke, Arnold Arluke, and Mike Michael	*The Sacrifice: How Scientific Experiments Transform Animals and People.* West Lafayette, IN: Purdue University Press, 2007.
P. Michael Conn and James V. Parker	*The Animal Research War.* New York: Palgrave Macmillan, 2008.
Ron Harré	*Pavlov's Dogs and Schrodinger's Cats: Scenes from the Living Laboratory.* New York: Oxford University Press, 2009.
Lynette A. Hart, Mary W. Wood, and Benjamin L. Hart	*Why Dissection?: Animal Use in Education.* Westport, CT: Greenwood Press, 2008.
Elizabeth Hess	*Nim Chimpsky: The Chimp Who Would Be Human.* New York: Bantam Books, 2008.
Linda Kalof and Amy J. Fitzgerald	*The Animals Reader: The Essential Classic and Contemporary Writings.* New York: Berg, 2007.
Lisa Kemmerer	*Sister Species: Women, Animals, and Social Justice.* Urbana, IL: University of Illinois Press, 2011.
Andrew Knight	*The Costs and Benefits of Animal Experiments.* New York: Palgrave Macmillan, 2011.

Vaughan Monamy *Animal Experimentation: A Guide to the Issues*. New York: Cambridge University Press, 2009.

Adrian R. Morrison *An Odyssey with Animals: A Veterinarian's Reflections on the Animal Rights and Welfare Debate*. New York: Oxford University Press, 2009.

The National Anti-Vivisection Society *A New Perspective: Seeking Justice for Animals Through the Power of Law*. Chicago: National Anti-Vivisection Society, 2008.

Wayne Pacelle *The Bond: Our Kinship with Animals, Our Call to Defend Them*. New York: William Morrow, 2011.

Allie Phillips *How Shelter Pets Are Brokered for Experimentation: Understanding Pound Seizure*. Lanham, MD, Rowman & Littlefield Publishers, 2010.

Deborah Rudacille *The Scalpel and the Butterfly: The War Between Animal Research and Animal Protection*. New York: Farrar, Straus and Giroux, 2000.

Matthew Scully *Dominion: The Power of Man, the Suffering of Animals, and the Call to Mercy*. New York: St. Martin's Press, 2002.

Robert Traer *Doing Environmental Ethics*. Boulder, CO: Westview Press, 2009.

Erin E. Williams and Margo DeMello

Why Animals Matter: The Case for Animal Protection. Amherst, NY: Prometheus Books, 2007.

Periodicals and Internet Sources

Neal Barnard

"Commentary on Institute of Medicine's Dec. 15 Chimpanzees in Biomedical and Behavioral Research Report," *Dr. Barnard's Blog*, December 30, 2011. www.pcrm.org.

Roscoe Bartlett

"Ending Experimentation on Chimpanzees Is Right Choice," *The Hill*, June 12, 2012.

BBC News

"University of Surrey Reveals it Tested 2500 Animals," May 24, 2012. www.bbc.co.uk.

Marc Bekoff

"One Small Step for Chimpanzeekind," *Huffington Post*, December 20, 2011. www.huffingtonpost.com.

P. Michael Conn

"Terrorism in the Name of Animal Rights," *Los Angeles Times*, November 12, 2008.

P. Michael Conn and James V. Parker

"Terrorizing Medical Research," *Washington Post*, December 8, 2008.

Daniel Cressey

"Noninvasive Medical Imaging Could Cut Lab Animal Use, Improve Data Quality," *Scientific American*, June 29, 2011.

Richard L. Cupp Jr.   "Bioethics and the Explosive Rise of Animal Law," *The American Journal of Bioethics*, November 5, 2009.

Laura Elder   "UTMB Shakes Up Animal Research Center," *Galveston County Daily News*, May 25, 2012.

Terrence Fisher   "Of Mice and Men: The Quest for More Accurate and Useful Animal Research Models," *BioNews*, August/September 2009.

Brandon Keim   "Hepatitis C: The Last Chimpanzee Research Battleground," *Wired*, November 14, 2011.

Brandon Keim   "NIH Accused of Dishonesty Over Chimp Research Plans," *Wired*, December 2, 2011.

Chris Magee   "We Need to Hear the Whole Truth About Animal Research," *Huffington Post*, June 7, 2012. www.huffingtonpost.com.

Peter Mansell   "Research Funders Call for Closer Attention to Guidelines on Reporting Animal Studies," *PharmaTimes*, May 22, 2012.

Nature   "Animal Rights and Wrongs," February 24, 2011.

New Internationalist Magazine   "Is Animal Testing Necessary to Advance Medical Research?," June 2011.

Malcolm Ritter   "Spinal Nerve Stimulation: Experiment Lets Spine-Injured Rats Walk, Climb," *Huffington Post*, May 31, 2012. www.huffingtonpost.com.

ScienceDaily   "Chimpanzees in Research: Statement on Institute of Medicine Report by NIH Director Francis Collins," December 15, 2011.

Kenneth P. Trevett   "Chimpanzee Research Must Continue—Here's Why," *The Hill*, May 21, 2012.

Paul Root Wolpe   "Ethical Limits to Bioengineering Animals," *Gene Watch*, April 2011.

David Wright   "'Zoobiquity': 7 Diseases Animals Share with Humans," *ABC News*, June 12, 2012. http://abcnews.go.com.

Index

A

Academic Medicine (magazine), 54

Acetaminophen studies, 21

Active seizure disorder, 17–18

Acute lymphoblastic leukemia (ALL), 12

Almay company, 90, 93

American Animal Hospital Association, 28

American Anti-Vivisection Society (AAVS), 19–25, 21, 91

American Cancer Association, 41

American College of Laboratory Animal Medicine (ACLAM), 32

American Psychiatric Association, 8

American Society for the Prevention of Cruelty to Animals (ASPCA), 85

American Veterinary Medical Association (AVMA), 29, 84

Americans for Medical Progress, 11–18

Angiogenesis, 44

Animal Care Panel, 33

Animal Enterprise Terrorism Act, 31

Animal experimentation

  alternatives to, 25

  animal care oversight, 31–34

  animal protection movement, 30–31, 34

  drug failure in, 22–23

  ethical concerns over, 20–21, 40

  expense of, 56

  flawed by design, 24

  isolation concerns, 7–8, 20, 50, 69, 73

  medical progress depends on, 11–18

  moral concerns, 38–39, 50

  overview, 7–10, 19–20

  recovery problems from, 23–24

  scientific limitations of, 21–24

  as unethical, 19–25

  See also Chimpanzees in research; Cosmetic testing on animals; Dogs and cats in research

Animal experimentation, elimination of

  challenges to, 54

  computer modeling, 56–58

  discussion and collaboration needs, 52–54

  end in sight, 47–48

  magnetic resonance imaging and, 59–60

  micro-dosing and, 58

  nonanimal methods *vs.*, 50–53

  oil dispersant safety, 46–47

  overview, 45–46, 49–50, 55–56

  priority of, 49–54

  replacement not completely possible, 55–60

  safety and speed concerns, 46

  through new technologies, 45–48

Animal Liberation (Singer), 86–87

Animal Liberation Front (ALF), 31, 88